495A 38

Rediscovering the Gift of Healing

LAWRENCE W. ALTHOUSE

NASHVILLE   ABINGDON

REDISCOVERING THE GIFT OF HEALING

Copyright © 1977 by Abingdon

Library of Congress Cataloging in Publication Data

ALTHOUSE, LAWRENCE W 1930-
  Rediscovering the gift of healing.

  Bibliography: p.
  1. Faith-cure. I. Title.
BT732.5.A46   615'.852   77-9290

ISBN 0-687-35860-4

MANUFACTURED BY THE PARTHENON PRESS AT NASHVILLE, TENNESSEE, UNITED STATES OF AMERICA

DEDICATION

This book is dedicated to all those who have helped me in my ministry of healing, many of whom have also encouraged me to write this book. To name only a few:

Ambrose and Olga Worrall
Spiritual Frontiers Fellowship
Dr. Alfred Price and the Order of St. Luke
Sid and Mary Council Crane
Gordon Turner
the Thursday morning group
Calvary Church
my parents and children
but most of all—my wife, Valere

Contents

Preface

Several years ago I arrived at a United Methodist church in suburban Kansas City to participate in a seminar on spiritual healing that was being held on the church premises, although not under the sponsorship of the church. As I walked up to the main entrance of the church, I found this sign on the door:

For Healing

Use the Back Door of the Church

I couldn't help musing that that is where healing has been for far too long. As I walked around to the back of the church, I renewed my avowed purpose of bringing the ministry of spiritual healing back into the mainstream of church life where I and many others believe it belongs.

If this book contributes in any way to the removal of that sign, I will be more than gratified.

Lawrence W. Althouse

CHAPTER 1

"Can You Help Me?"

I've received many wonderful Christmas cards over the years, but none so exciting and joyous as one from a young woman whom I had never met. It was Christmas Eve, and the mailman had just deposited in our box the last delivery we would receive until after Christmas. The mail seemed hardly worth the trip to the door: several bills, an advertisement, and one envelope that obviously contained an almost belated Christmas greeting.

The postmark indicated a town somewhere in Minnesota, and I couldn't imagine who might possibly be sending me this greeting. Upon opening it, however, I found a name that had become very familiar to me and to the prayer group that met with me on Thursday mornings. It was signed "Lorraine Alt."

Nine months before, I had received my first communication from Lorraine. It came one day in the mail in the same way many such requests have arrived for healing prayer. Lorraine had seen the name of my church on the back of *Sharing* (the official magazine of the Order of St. Luke the Physician) in a listing of churches that pursue a healing ministry. We were probably only one of a number of churches that received the same pitiful request. At any rate, Lorraine, a young woman in her mid twenties, wrote me from a mental hospital where she was a patient. She was desperately ill, she said, and her depression seemed to know no limitations. If she soon didn't receive help, she indicated, she could not survive. "Can you help me?" she wanted to know.

The letter in my hands fairly crackled with anguish, and I sat down immediately to write a reply. Could we help her? I was sure that we could, although I couldn't promise anything; for, I said, "God alone is the healer." We would put her on our prayer list and "send healing" to her each Thursday when we had our weekly healing service in the sanctuary of my church.

7

The next Thursday morning, I shared the letter with our prayer group, and several women of the group indicated that they would write her letters of encouragement. We prayed for her that morning, asking that God's will would be done so that Lorraine might again be whole: mind, body, and spirit.

We did not hear from Lorraine again in the months that followed, but about a month after I received her letter, I heard from a woman in Minnesota who said she was a very close friend of Lorraine's. It was a brief, terse note thanking us for our efforts but advising us that we could stop praying for Lorraine because doctors had confided that there was nothing that could be done for her. Lorraine would probably die soon, her friend predicted gloomily.

For most of the rest of the year we heard nothing from or about Lorraine. Still, we did not take her name off the prayer list, and her healing was a weekly concern for the group and even a daily concern for some of us. As time went on, however, I began to wonder whether there was any point in continuing to pray for her. For all I knew, she might be dead by this time.

It was then that I received Lorraine's Christmas Eve greeting. It was not a note from one about to expire! Apologizing for the tardiness of the card, Lorraine went on to say:

> I'd like my friends at Calvary to know I was released from the State Hospital here on May 22. I want to thank all of you, for I know it was through the prayers of my friends and relatives that God gave me salvation, healed me of mental illness and filled me with his Holy Spirit. Glory to God!

I still have Lorraine's card, and each Christmas I like to read it again. It still has the power to inspire me and recharge my faith, as well as to renew my commitment to the ministry of spiritual healing.

Since that time I have received great numbers of letters, telegrams, and telephone calls, asking, in one way or another, "Can you help me?" Each time my answer has been the same: "I cannot promise the results you look for, only that I will do my

8

best, confident in the knowledge of the many people who have been greatly helped by this ministry." [1]

Some of my co-workers in the ministry of healing have often characterized my healing ministry as "soft sell and low-key." I have kept it that way, for the most part, because I remember all too vividly my own disgust and repugnance when, as a seminary student, I attended a healing service in a tent pitched on the old circus grounds in Reading, Pennsylvania. I suppose I was somewhat cynical to begin with, but what I saw there that evening—the hysteria, the careful manipulation of people's emotions, the unsubstantiated claims, and the obvious failures—slammed the door of my own receptivity for the next decade of my ministerial career. In my mind the healing ministry was tragically linked with hysteria, deception, and fraud. I saw no place for it in the life of the church.

Ten years later I realized that the ministry of healing had a legitimate place in the mission of the church and that it did not have to be anything like the debacle I had witnessed as a seminary student. As the old saying goes, I had thrown the baby out with the bath water, something the church has frequently done, to its own detriment.

I shudder to think of the joys and inspiration that I would have missed in these past ten years if I had continued to believe that the ministry of healing was neither valid nor honest.

I remember vividly the young German woman who came to one of my first healing services. She had just recently joined my church, and when I looked up from the lectern I was surprised to see her numbered among the ten or eleven sitting quietly in the sanctuary. She seemed healthy enough; in fact, her constantly red cheeks indicated a kind of breathless vitality and wholeness. Furthermore, she had not seemed "the kind of person" who would come to a healing service. (In those days I was unduly impressed with a kind of "sheep and goats" mentality when it came to who would or would not be receptive.) I couldn't help but wonder what she would think of this service which in all probability had no parallel in her native German *Landeskirche*, or "state church."

9

I shook off those thoughts as I began what was beginning to be a familiar order of worship. I began with "Words of Preparation":

"Come to me, all who labor and are heavy laden, and I will give you rest."

"For where two or three are gathered in my name, there am I in the midst of them."

"My peace I give to you."

"Ask, and it will be given you; seek, and you will find; knock, and it will be opened to you."

"If you ask anything in my name, I will do it."

These familiar promises I followed with a prayer of invocation known to many Christians of diverse denominations, "Almighty God, unto whom all hearts are open, all desires known," ending with the Lord's Prayer.

From Psalms I spoke familiar words as a call to confession:

While I refused to speak, my body wasted away
with my moaning all day long.
For day and night
thy hand was heavy upon me,
the sap in me dried up as in a summer drought.
Then I declared my sin, I did not conceal my guilt.
I said, "With sorrow I will confess
my disobedience to the Lord";
then thou didst remit the penalty of my sin. (32:3–5 NEB)

Asking the tiny congregation to examine their consciences in silence, I led them in a familiar prayer of general confession: "Almighty and most merciful Father, we have erred and strayed from thy ways like lost sheep."

Following a scriptural assurance of pardon, we sang a hymn, "Breathe on Me, Breath of God," after which I read a scripture lesson and gave a brief homily on an incident in Jesus' healing ministry.

One of the women who came to the healing service each week walked quietly down the aisle to the altar rail and handed me a legal-sized tablet. Placing the tablet on the altar, I led the people in a prayer of intercession, reading aloud the names on the tablet.

A simple invitation was given to come forward for "the laying on of hands for the healing of mind, body, and spirit, either for yourself or in intercession for another." Helga, the German girl, did not hesitate; getting up from her pew, she walked forward and kneeled before me at the altar rail.

Some people tell me for what or whom they want to pray, but Helga bowed her head and said nothing. When I lay my hands upon someone for healing, I ask Christ to work God's will through me, and then, in a sense, I try to get out of the way. I don't mean I make my mind a blank at that time, but I think of nothing in particular, letting my consciousness float, as it were, yielding myself so that Christ may work as he pleases.

I cannot say how long I leave my hands on the patient, but when I feel that the "treatment" is over, I pray a brief prayer aloud for the patient, a prayer of praise and thanksgiving for what has been received.

When I said amen and removed my hands from her head, Helga smiled at me and left the sanctuary. It was only a few days later at a Sunday worship service that she revealed to me what had happened. She had come to the healing service because of a terrible toothache. Having been informed that she could not see her dentist until the next day, she came with the determination of finding relief at the healing service. It hardly surprised her that while my hands were upon her head, the agonizing toothache went away completely. She had expected that it would happen, she said, and it did.

I think too of a middle-aged woman in my congregation who called me one evening and said: "Larry, you've got to get over here right away. The doctor says that if Clarence's fever does not break in the next half hour, he'll have to put Clarence in the hospital. You know we just can't have that!" Mary Catherine was not the kind of person you argued with, and I dropped what I was doing and drove quickly to their apartment.

Clarence looked terribly ill. Without wasting any time in

preliminaries, Mary Catherine said, "Put your hands on Clarence; I know he's going to be healed right now!" I marveled at her determination and thought of the Phoenician woman who persisted with Jesus until he healed her daughter.

Often the patient feels heat from my hands, but this time my hands fairly flinched when they touched Clarence's head. It was very hot. After about five minutes I prayed, committing Clarence to Christ's healing will, and left. As I was walking in the door at the parsonage, the phone was ringing; it was Mary Catherine. Her voice was just a shade beyond matter of fact: "You'll be glad to know that Clarence's temperature went down to normal within five minutes after you left. I just knew it would."

I think also of another late-night call, this one from the mother of a little girl of eight. Doreen had been taken to the hospital with respiratory problems and a very high temperature. For an hour, her mother told me, Doreen had been delirious, thrashing about the bed, moaning, and crying. Worst of all, she would let no one near her but her mother. "Can't you do something?" her mother wanted to know. "Let's put her in Christ's hands, Mrs. Bryers, and see what can be done," I answered.

Privately, I was concerned. I didn't know how I was going to place my hands on Doreen with her thrashing about as she was. But I reached over and let my hands move with her as she tossed back and forth. I tried to pray aloud, but I had difficulty with Doreen's moaning. At last, I said amen and removed my hands. Stepping back from the bed a few paces, I was amazed to see a change come over Doreen. She was lying still; she wasn't moaning any longer! She smiled weakly and then closed her eyes to sleep. The next morning Doreen's parents called to say that she had passed the crisis and was beginning to feel fine.

I treasure a letter that I received from a Michigan gentleman several years ago after returning from a large public healing service in Chicago. Hundreds of people came forward and received prayer and the laying on of hands from approximately twenty healers standing at the front of the theater.

Mr. Shirmer was one of the people who had come forward for

healing, although I did not remember him. In his letter he reminded me:

> I told you that the hearing in both ears was seemingly impaired, you covered my ears with your hands, and after blessing me, sent me on my way.
>
> I have used a hearing aid for the past few years, but since this treatment I have not put it back on. My friends tell me they no longer have to raise their voices when talking to me.
>
> This letter is an expression of my thanks to Almighty God for the healing which has taken place through your ministration, and you may use it in any way in which it might be helpful in the healing of others.[2]

Of course, spiritual healing is not always that sudden and dramatic. In fact, the dramatic, instantaneous healing is the exception, not the rule. Most patients who receive healing usually experience their improvement over a period of time, often a fairly long period of time. Usually, it requires more than just one visit to the healing service. There are those, of course, who say, "I went to a healing service once, but I wasn't cured." Of course not; nor do many people go to a physician just once and expect to be healed.

If there is any apparent difference between the healing ministry that Jesus practiced and the ministry of healing that is pursued in many churches today, it is that although all or most of Jesus' healings seemed to be immediate, in the healing ministry today that kind of healing is not common. That is hardly an adequate reason for ignoring this ministry, no more than we would stop praying because we seldom pray with either the power or the results with which Jesus prayed.

This may be illustrated by one of the most gratifying cases that is in my files. Henry Gibson appeared at our healing service one day, a stranger to all of us, although we were becoming accustomed to that. His wife who worked near the church told him of our Thursday service, and, desperate, he decided to give it a try.

Henry had contracted myasthenia gravis early in 1973 although it was not diagnosed until February, 1974. He had been

13

in two different hospitals four different times, and his prognosis, said the experts, was not favorable. A thymectomy was suggested, but since he had a history of gall bladder trouble, he declined it. He was then placed on a rather dangerous medicine (with possible bad side effects) and became an outpatient, reporting every week at first and then every two weeks. On a visit to his specialist in mid March, he was told that there was no apparent improvement, and he went home discouraged, with an appointment to return in two weeks. Mr. Gibson relates what happened next in his own words:

The following Saturday morning about 8:25 a.m. I was looking through *TV Guide* and saw a listing at 8:30 for Kathryn Kuhlman [a well-known charismatic healer]. Something made me turn on the program and much to my surprise her guests that day were a mother who had taught nursing and her young son—both having received a healing from myasthenia gravis at one of Miss Kuhlman's services. My wife . . . suggested that I might want to fly out to Pittsburgh and attend one of Miss Kuhlman's [services]. Traveling presented a great problem because I had great difficulty in speaking and swallowing and it was necessary to have a diet of liquid or extremely soft foods. I was determined to attend your healing services with my wife as soon as possible. When the time came that I could do so, I attended weekly for about four weeks but felt no better. Then in one of your services you said, "You must believe you are healed" and I did. That day when I came forward for the laying-on-of-hands, I felt an extremely warm sensation in the middle of my shoulders where you had placed your hand. During the week [following] the extreme salivation that had bothered me, eased and my swallowing was slightly better.

You were out of town when the next healing service was held and when I came forward for the laying-on-of-hands, Rev. William Kreichbaum who was conducting the service placed his hands on each side of my throat. Again I had the sensation of extreme warmth, where his hands had touched. . . . The following week I made rapid progress and the next time my physician saw me, he was quite surprised with my improvement. He decreased the frequency of my medication and was so pleased with my condition that I was told that I did not have to return for two months. . . . I now . . . can swallow regular food and my speech is almost normal.

I am so very thankful that the Lord has seen fit to guide me,

14

through you, in accepting his wonderful healing power and I feel
that I must let everyone know about it and hope that those who
need healing will BELIEVE as I did. If they do, many blessings
are waiting for them just for the taking.[3]

Henry Gibson's case illustrates two important factors. One of
these is that the healer and the healee must be patient and
persistent. Usually, healing takes time, just as getting sick usually
takes time.

Second, the ministry of spiritual healing is not carried on in
competition with physicians, nor is it an alternative to the practice
of medicine. On the card that served as an order of worship for our
healing service we printed this instruction: "It is important to
cooperate with your doctor and follow his directions. Do not take
it upon yourself to cease his prescribed medications and
treatments. Let him pronounce you well."

Mr. Gibson obviously is firmly convinced that his healing was
due to what happened in our healing services. I will not make that
claim, for it is impossible to prove just why or how he was healed.
To me it doesn't matter who or what gets the credit. God alone
was the healer, whether he used a physician and his medications
or two clergyman healers or even all of us. The most important
thing is that Mr. Gibson had reached a point of despair about his
condition, and soon he was well or almost at the end of his
recovery. With the man born blind he can share in that same
conviction: "One thing I know, that though I was blind, now I
see" (John 9:25)!

CHAPTER 2

"What's a Guy Like You Doing in a Thing Like This?"

Accordingly you should proceed as follows: Go to him [a sick man] with your curate and two or three good men. Confident that you as pastor of the place are clothed with the authority of the ministerial office, lay your hands upon him and say, "Peace be with you, dear brother, from God our Father, and from our Lord Jesus Christ. . . . Then, when you depart, lay your hands upon the man and say once more: "These signs shall follow them that believe: they shall lay hands on the sick and they shall recover." Do this again—even up to three times a day.

—Martin Luther in a letter to the pastor at Belgern

I was in the midst of making my rounds in the hospital. As I was getting off the elevator I came face to face with another local pastor. Our respective pastorates were in adjoining suburbs, but we seldom saw each other except for ministers' meetings and occasions like this in the hospitals.

Unless we were there for an emergency, three to five minutes of good-natured and meaningless banter was customary. I must confess I would often have preferred to duck these clerical hospital encounters, for the level of conversation never rose much above "And how big was *your* congregation on Easter?" Clergy, it seems, seldom say anything important to one another, reserving such matters presumably for their congregations.

After a few moments of innocuous clergy talk, my colleague looked warily to either side—as if to see who might be within hearing distance—lowered his voice, and said, "Uh, Larry, do you—do you still have—uh—those uh—healing services on Thursday morning?" There was nothing wrong with the content of his question, but the tone and manner with which he asked it reminded me of someone asking another whether he was still beating his wife or hitting the bottle.

When I replied in the affirmative, he said nothing but smiled wanly and nodded his head as if affirming something quite difficult to comprehend. I could hear him saying to himself, "Son of a gun, he really does have a healing service, just like they said!"

During the first five or six years of my healing ministry the above incident was about par for the course when it came to the reactions of fellow clergy in the area to my weekly healing service. They seldom mentioned it, and, if they did, it was usually in a semihushed, conspiratorial tone. It was as if they were saying to me, "Don't worry, my friend, your secret is safe with me"!

Only one of them, a longtime friend, spoke candidly to me, "Larry, what's a guy like you doing in a thing like this?" I knew what the *like you* meant; I had the reputation of being more intellectual than emotional in my religious style, theologically more liberal than fundamental, inclined to approach any religious matter from a rational perspective. (One of the minor benefits of my healing ministry is that when it comes to my theology my colleagues and others no longer know how to classify me; none of their labels seem to fit!)

The *like this* indicated that, because he thought we shared the same theological label, he assumed that we would both disdain the practice of spiritual healing. And, up until some time in the early 1960s he would have been quite correct. As I have already indicated in chapter 1, my seminary days' experience with a tent-meeting faith healer had soured me on this whole subject. In the years that followed, there was nothing to change my conviction that faith healing was a harmful fraud.

Then, sometime during 1962, I was introduced to an amazing couple who would soon cause me to reconsider my whole perspective on this matter. The couple were an aeronautical engineer, Ambrose Worrall, and his wife, Olga. I was persuaded by a mutual friend, a Presbyterian minister, to seek them out. If the suggestion had come from almost anyone else, I would hardly have acted upon it, for I was inclined to be very hostile to the idea of spiritual healing. But because I deeply respected my friend, a man whom I knew was theologically solid, I agreed to try to approach the Worralls with an open mind.

I only partly kept my promise. Upon meeting the Worralls I was no more receptive to the idea of healing than I had been, but I was very much impressed by Ambrose and Olga Worrall themselves. First of all, their attitude was so different from what I had expected. They were not wild-eyed emotionalists, and I was even more surprised to find that they accepted no monetary or material remuneration of any kind for their healing work which was being carried on in a quiet, dignified manner in a Baltimore United Methodist church. If they weren't commercializing their healing ministry, what was their motive? It was soon apparent that here were two people who recognized a special God-given gift and were deeply committed to employing it in the service of Christ for the benefit of their fellowmen.

Most surprising, however, was Ambrose's explanation of his healing gift from a scientific perspective. He spoke not of the supernatural but of an "energy flow" from God through the healer to the healee. He told of experiments conducted in scientific laboratories that suggested that both he and Olga were conductors of an unknown but not supernatural energy that often was able to produce startling results with patients, particularly those judged hopeless by their physicians. I was amazed to hear Olga tell of the doctors who called them from time to time for assistance with patients who were not responding to medical therapy (something that I too would experience years later in my own ministry).

I was not at all convinced about spiritual healing, but because I was so impressed with Ambrose and Olga Worrall, I agreed to rethink the whole subject, both theologically and scientifically. Olga suggested some books to read, but, most important of all, she suggested that I reread relevant New Testament passages in the Bible.

It is dangerous for a Christian to reapproach the Bible with the commitment to an open mind—particularly a minister! Who knows what God might be able to say to us if we give him that opportunity? Nevertheless, I decided to try to do just that.

I was more than a little amazed at what I found. For one thing, I was surprised at how pervasive the healing ministry was in the Four Gospels. My rough calculations indicated that approximately one fifth of Matthew, Mark, Luke, and John are concerned with Jesus' healing ministry. I had always been aware of this aspect of Jesus' ministry, but I suppose that whenever I had previously read these passages I had tended to skip over them with a slight attack of twentieth-century embarassment. Now it was evident to me that the healing ministry was at the very heart of Jesus' mission (see Matt. 4:23, 9:35; Acts 10:38).

Furthermore, I was surprised to find that the scriptural basis for an ongoing ministry of healing was very sound. I found Jesus sending out his disciples to "preach, teach, and heal" (see Matt. 10:5–8; Mark 6:7–13; Luke 9:1–6; 10:1–20). I found that rather than expiring with the death and resurrection of Jesus the healing ministry continued on into the Apostolic Church (see Acts 3, 4, 9, 14, 16, 20, 22, 28). If healing was to be limited to Jesus' earthly ministry as the messianic Son of God, as many indicate today, the apostles must not have realized it!

In fact, the Gospel According to John indicates that Jesus led his disciples to expect to continue his miracles: "Truly, truly, I say to you, he who believes in me will also do the works that I do; and greater works than these will he do" (14:12). Paul listed healing as one of the specific gifts of the Spirit in I Corinthians 12:9, and the apostle James makes a point to instruct the church: "Is any among you sick? Let him call for the elders of the church, and let them pray over him, anointing him with oil in the name of the Lord; and the prayer of faith will save the sick man, and the Lord will raise him up" (James 5:14–15).

Nor, I found, was the ministry of healing limited to the Apostolic Age. Returning to church history, I found that it prevailed through the first three centuries of Christianity and even beyond that, although the rise of the professional clergy shifted the emphasis from a charismatic to a sacramental ministry. We find significant references to the healing ministry among such church fathers as Theophilus of Antioch, the Shepherd of Hermas, Irenaeus, Tertulian, Origen, and Justin Martyr.

Another indication of the part healing played in the early church is the competition between the churches and the healing shrines of Aesculapius (the Greek god whose shrines greatly influenced the great Hippocratic school of medicine). Morton T. Kelsey tells us:

> It was not by chance that Christian churches came to be regarded as healing shrines competitive with the shrines of Aesculapius. It was also natural that in many places the Christian churches should take over the function of those temples as the pagan religion died out, and that a Christian shrine often appeared on the site of a former pagan temple.[1]

My research into the place of healing in early Christianity also gave me a different concept of the mission of the church. I knew, of course, that the gospel was the good news of salvation, but I was to learn that my concept of the meaning of *salvation* was distorted. Salvation, I had assumed, dealt only with the spirit of persons, not their bodies. But my research reminded me of the Hebrew concept of man as a totality of mind, body, and spirit. I remembered that the idea that the spirit needed to be liberated from the evil body was a Greek not a Hebrew concept. Jesus did not come to save disembodied spirits but whole men and women. Jesus did not teach or even suggest that the spirit is good and the body evil. These prejudices against the body came from Platonic and Stoic sources, and, in the time of the early church, from Manichaean heresy.

Still, in time, the heresy began to prevail, and gradually the church adopted the view that the flesh was evil. Subsequently, there began to grow in the church an attitude toward the body that gave high value to the various means of mortifying the flesh. Crucifixion came to be more highly regarded than resurrection.

Along with this view there arose a growing conviction that illness represents God's punishment and chastisement of the sinful. Morton Kelsey wonders whether this increased valuation of physical suffering as well as the growing "disapproval of

easing the pains of the flesh'' weren't, in fact, an alibi for the loss
of the healing gift in the church. Under the influence of Pope
Gregory a profound change had taken place by the eighth century:

> Western thinking about healing had come full circle. Sickness was
> no longer understood as the malicious work of "demons" or the
> Evil One, to be countered in every instance. Instead, it was the
> mark of God's correction, sometimes inflicted by the negative
> powers with his approval, to bring moral renewal. There was no
> question of God's *power* to heal or his ability to intervene, but only
> of his *will* to heal. Only the righteous were likely to find healing.
> We find in Gregory's attitude the theme that grew more and more
> prevalent in the West until it was fully expressed in the English
> Office of the Visitation of the Sick. Here the Old Testament view
> of sickness largely displaced that of Jesus, the apostles, the early
> church, and the eastern church.[2]

Father Francis MacNutt believes that this influence was further
reinforced in recent centuries by Cartesian and Jansenist
influences, especially in the French and the Irish-Roman
churches, stressing "a dualism in man, with spirit and mind being
seen as noble while the body is, at best, a necessary evil."[3]
MacNutt sees in the church today, however, a growing return to
the view of humanity that Jesus held: the person as a totality of
mind, body, and spirit, all valuable in God's sight, all a valid
concern of the church's ministry.

Furthermore, I found that the Greek word *sozo,* which in
English we invariably translate as "to save," may just as rightly
be translated as "to heal or make whole" and that the Greek word
soter means both "savior" (as we usually translate it in English)
and "healer."[4] Thus *salvation* does not mean simply the rescue
of the spirit but the bringing of wholeness to heal wherever we are
broken. (It is interesting that the German word *heilen* also means
"to save, to heal, to make whole.")

Christ's ministry, therefore—as well as that of his church—
is a healing, saving ministry that seeks to restore wholeness to
mind, body, and spirit. He came to bring healing to broken minds,
broken spirits, broken bodies, broken lives, broken families,
broken communities, and died to heal a broken world. Jesus' own

characterizations of his messianic mission indicate this same concern for our physical as well as our spiritual brokenness:

> He opened the book and found the place where it was written,
> "The Spirit of the Lord is upon me,
> because he has anointed me to preach good news to the poor.
> He has sent me to proclaim release to the captives
> and recovering of sight to the blind,
> to set at liberty those who are oppressed,
> to proclaim the acceptable year of the Lord." . . .
> And he began to say to them, "Today this scripture has been fulfilled in your hearing." (Luke 4:17–21)

And when John the Baptist's emissaries came to Jesus with their disturbing question, "Are you he who is to come, or shall we look for another?" see how Jesus answers:

> Go and tell John what you hear and see: the blind receive their sight and the lame walk, lepers are cleansed and the deaf hear, and the dead are raised up, and the poor have good news preached to them." (Matt. 11:2–6)

And when Jesus gives his yardstick for discipleship in the parable of the last judgment (Matt. 25:31–46), the emphasis is on the physical plight of "the least of these"—their hunger, thirst, nakedness, sickness, and imprisonment. This is not to demean the importance of the spirit, but simply to indicate that when we emphasize *only* the ministry to the spirit, we ignore the meaning of *salvation* as found in the Four Gospels. Too long have we ignored the mind and the body, and the ministry of the church has distorted the meaning of the good news. Thus Alan Richardson has written:

> The success of Christianity as a missionary religion in the ancient world . . . was in no small part due to its preaching of the Healer-Saviour who satisfied a need which the old gods could not meet; and it is highly significant that the last of these gods to go down before Christianity was Æsculapius, a god of healing.[5]

Theologian Paul Tillich also lifts up this perspective that is often either overlooked or rationalized: "The tremendous importance which the healing stories have in the New Testament records is understandable only if one knows that the Kingdom of God was supposed to come as a healing power on earth." [6]

One instructive indication of what had happened in the church since the Apostolic Age, I discovered, is to be found in the Roman Catholic Church's sacrament of unction. I knew that Holy Unction was the sacrament of last rites performed by the priest for the dying. But Olga Worrall told me that unction had begun as a sacrament of healing. "Look it up for yourself," she challenged me, apparently sensing my cynicism.

I was surprised with what I found. Originally, modeled on the admonition in the Epistle of James (5:13–15), it was intended as a sacrament for physical healing. Later, under the influence of Jerome and Gregory, as physical suffering was now regarded with favor, the sacrament gradually lost its significance for physical healing and replaced this with a spiritual purpose—to prepare the soul in danger of imminent death for entrance into the glory beyond. Along with this change in purpose there was a change in name to Last Annointing, or Extreme Unction. In time the term *Last Unction* came to be associated with the last act performed in preparing a person for death. What an ironic twist—from healing to dying! No wonder Roman Catholics were frightened by the appearance of the priest with his flask of oil!

Today, however, we see a change that has taken place since Vatican II. It is no longer called Extreme Unction but Holy Unction, or Annointing of the Sick, and it is regarded once again as a sacrament of healing, not of preparation for death. According to Vatican liturgical expert Father Secondo Mazzarello: "The aim now is to comfort the sick person. Pain and sickness are seen as the problems of the entire man, body and soul together. The new rite gets away from the Platonic concept, which for centuries split man into body and soul." [7]

My reappraisal of the healing ministry in light of the Bible, church history, and theology brought a gradual but profound change in my attitude. No less significant was the reappraisal I made of my scientific world view (of which we will say more in chapter 4). My prejudices crumbled, and I began to accept not only the possibility of the healing ministry in the church but also its validity and necessity.

All that remained was the need to match experience with my new attitude. Thus, I began to attend as often as I could the Thursday healing service held by the Worralls and the Rev. Robert Kirkley at the Mount Washington United Methodist Church in Baltimore, and, at Olga's suggestion, I also visited the weekly healing service of the Rev. Dr. Alfred Price, rector of St. Stephen's Episcopal Church in Philadelphia and warden of the Order of St. Luke the Physician. Watching them and those who came to their services, I concluded that here at last was being demonstrated the New Testament power that so many of us talked about but seldom witnessed!

One day following the healing service, Olga said to me, "You have the gift of healing, you know, and the time has come for you to start a healing service in your own church." I was as overwhelmed by that suggestion as I had been years before when someone suggested I ought to consider the Christian ministry. I really didn't know how to argue with her; so I went home and brooded until, at last, I was convinced that God had spoken through her and truly wanted me to begin a healing ministry at Calvary Church.

I thought about it, prayed about it, and agonized over it, but the conviction never diminished; it only got stronger. At last I took courage in hand and approached the official board of my church and proposed this new ministry for our church. To my surprise, the proposal was approved almost without discussion and no dissent.

Thus, on Thursday morning, January 13, 1966, I held my first healing service. I was possessed of two emotions that morning. On the one hand, I was scared stiff. I felt that I didn't know what I was doing and couldn't help wondering what my church would think, what the community would think, and, maybe most of all, what my fellow clergy would think of me. (As it was, my fears were justified, at least at first.) But the other feeling was a conviction that I was doing precisely what God had called me to do.

In time the former emotion diminished, and the latter increased and became even more certain. There has never been a more important decision in my whole ministry than to begin the ministry of spiritual healing.

So, today when people ask or, more likely, imply, "What's a guy like you doing in a thing like that?" I think of the story I heard about Thoreau. In prison for one of his numerous causes, Thoreau was discovered by a friend who exclaimed, "Thoreau, what are you doing in there?" Retorted Thoreau, "My friend, what are you doing out there?"

CHAPTER 3

The Scandal About God's Will

We pray, not in order to alter His will, but to bring ourselves into accordance with it.

—*Emily Gardner Neal,* The Lord Is Our Healer

It has never been my intention to produce a theology of spiritual healing. But one cannot long be engaged in the healing ministry without theologizing on this subject to some degree. It is quite unavoidable.

What makes it unavoidable are the questions that come both from others and from oneself. The ministry of healing is bound to raise difficult questions, and it is in trying to arrive at sincere and thoughtful answers to those questions that we find ourselves working out a theology.

One of the problems with the term *theology* is that it evokes overtones of tedium and boredom. Many of us feel about theology the way we feel about calisthenics: we know it must be good for us, but we'd prefer if someone else were to do it for us.

Theology, however, is not intended to be boring; although, unfortunately, that's what theologians tend to make it. Theology is actually intended to be our attempt to think through our religious experience and communicate it to others.

That's what my theology of spiritual healing represents—an honest attempt to bring some understanding into this experience and to communicate that understanding to others so that it may be beneficial to them. It makes no pretensions as *systematic theology* in the usual sense of that term. It is incomplete, and there are holes in it. At most, it is a kind of operating hypothesis, a set of reasoned assumptions upon which my ministry of healing is based, my attempts over the years to answer the disturbing questions I must ask myself or have been asked by others.

There is probably no question asked more frequently in the ministry of healing than that of God's will. It takes many different forms:

What did I do to deserve this?

Why does God allow my child to suffer like this?

Pastor, is this condition of mine God's will, do you think?

Apparently God doesn't intend for me to get well, does he?

The questions are always an attempt to put together two seemingly contradictory realities: the evil of illness and the goodness of God.

A number of years ago I was walking across a busy intersection when I heard the scream of an auto's brakes behind me. Swinging around, I turned in time to see a large truck strike a little boy who had darted into the street. A crowd quickly gathered, but it was immediately apparent that the little boy was dead. As his sobbing mother threw herself across his body, I heard someone trying to comfort her: "Mary, don't blame yourself, it was God's will!"

I did not know the people, but it was with great difficulty that I restrained myself from challenging that terrible blasphemy. "God's will"? To crush the life out of a little child and snatch him from his mother and father? After thousands of years of religious ecstacy and revelation, of study and contemplation, is *that* the best answer we can give?

I think not. And, I suppose I've always felt that way, but it wasn't until I began my ministry of healing that that conviction was so strongly reconfirmed. One of the first patients who came to me for help was a man with crippling arthritis. He was a humble and devout man. If one were to believe that illness is decreed by a legalistic God to those who fail to measure up in terms of morality and faith, this man would have seemed to be one of the least likely to be selected for so painful and limiting a disease.

Having suffered painfully for many years, he came to me as a last resort. That he wanted to be well again was obvious, but I could also discern that there was something else that was bothering him. At last he verbalized it: "Pastor, is it possible that it is God's will for me to be like this?" If God wanted him to be ill

27

for the sake of some divine purpose, what reason was there for him to seek healing?

I have often marveled at the irony of those who tell you blithely that it must be God's will for them to be ill and then march off to the doctor's office to seek therapy. Why would anyone go to a doctor to be healed if he or she believed that the illness was a manifestation of the will of God?

In making a thorough study of Jesus' ministry of healing in the Gospels, I came to the realization that Jesus apparently never questioned whether it might be God's will for someone to be ill. If God does will for some people to be ill and for others to be healthy, wouldn't Jesus have been taking a terrible risk in giving healing to all who came to him?

Yet there is nowhere in the Gospels that Jesus ever refuses to give healing to someone on the grounds that it is God's will for that person to be ill. Remembering the multitudes that came to him with their infirmities, wouldn't it be amazing to think that only those who were intended to be well came to him for healing? *Apparently Jesus never questions whether it might be God's will to heal someone, because he believes it is God's will for all his children to be whole.* Not once does he pray for healing, saying, "If it be your will, Lord." Actually, there is only one place in all the Gospels where Jesus prays in that manner—the garden of Gethsemane—and that prayer has nothing to do with healing or health. Why then has this caveat become so much a part of our prayers for healing? If Jesus never doubts that it is God's will for us to be whole, why should we?

A thorough search of the Gospels destroys another of our rationalizations about God's will and wholeness: Jesus never makes moral worth a condition for healing. He never says: "I'm sorry, but I will not heal you because you are not worthy. Go and clean up your life so that you may deserve God's healing love." As Morton T. Kelsey puts it, "Nowhere in the gospels is there any suggestion of Jesus asking a sick person what he had done or whether he had sinned before healing him."[1]

People frequently question whether they are "worthy" to ask God for healing. But personal worth was never a factor in Jesus' ministry. He healed people whom his contemporaries judged to be quite unworthy of healing. In fact, it must be evident that healing is always a matter of grace. It is undeserved yet available to all who will accept it. To be sure, after Jesus healed he sometimes told the patient to "go and sin no more" But that command always *followed* rather than preceded the healing.

Furthermore, as we study his ministry in the Gospels, we do not find him ever suggesting that God intends for a person to be ill in order to grow in faith, patience, or any other virtue. Asked for healing, Jesus never responds with, "I'm sorry, but this illness will be good for you; it'll be good for your character," as we are sometimes tempted to pontificate.

Actually, the goodness of illness is another of our popular assumptions that is not substantiated in the Gospels. If illness is sometimes something "good" for us, one never gains that impression from Jesus. No matter what the circumstances may be, Jesus never regards illness in a friendly manner. Morton Kelsey in *Healing and Christianity* points out that Jesus' underlying and consistent attitude toward illness is always one of opposition.

> Sickness and demon possession were considered prime evidences of evil in the world. By dealing with them as the Messiah, the agent of God, Jesus laid the attitude of God toward sickness out on the counter where all could see it. . . .
> Jesus' underlying attitude was that the demon-possessed and the physically ill were under the influence and control of an evil power.[2]

It is a fallacy to believe that illness is good for us or that it naturally brings the best out of us. Any one who works around sick people knows that they are rarely at their best. In fact, most of us are at our worst when we are ill. As Emily Gardner Neal has observed:

> Illness does not tend to sanctify the sufferer, but quite the reverse.
> I have seen that physical suffering is not inclined to elevate the

spirit, but in the majority of cases degrades its victims to a purely animalistic level where the only reality is pain, and the only desire its alleviation. . . .

A nagging headache or a bad cold tends to ruin the best of dispositions; and if you are like most of us, Christian or not, and have ever suffered even a severe toothache, your chief interest at the time was probably in reaching the dentist—not the Kingdom.[3]

Why then this persistent belief that sickness is "good for us"? Because, although illness is an evil, even it can be transformed into something good if we turn to God. Thus, the "good" is not something that is inherent in it but something that can be infused into it by a loving, redeeming God. God can make something creative of any of our failures, sins, or tragedies if we will open ourselves to him. But that does not mean that we shall praise evil because of the good that God can bring forth from it. As Paul puts it, "Are we to continue in sin that grace may abound? By no means!" (Rom. 6:1).

If, then, God wills for us to be whole, why is there sickness in the world? Obviously, although God may will wholeness, there is sickness and physical misery all around us. What explanation can there be unless God wills it?

There is an answer, I believe. *Illness is part of the price that we pay for our free will.* God wills wholeness for all his children, but he has also given us free will, and the two are often locked in mortal combat.

Many who are in doubt over the question of God's will for wholeness would never entertain those same doubts when it comes to righteousness. We are convinced that God always wills for us to be righteous, never to be sinful, weak, or evil. Nevertheless, none of us is ever fully or consistently righteous. One of the central beliefs of the Christian faith is that "none is righteous, no, not one" (Rom. 3:10).

So how do we explain our ability to sin in the face of our conviction that God wills us to be righteous? The best explanation, it seems, is our free will. God wills us to be righteous, but he gives us free will, and therefore he permits us to choose to sin instead. Thus, if I drive carelessly and kill a

30

pedestrian, if I embezzle the firm's funds and am apprehended, I will not turn to God and cry, "Oh, God, how could you let this happen?" For I will know how it happened. I made my own choices for good and evil, and I alone am responsible. God may will my righteousness, but he does not compel me to do his will.

Might we not apply this same reasoning to the question of wholeness and illness? Can we not also say that God wills for us to be whole, but he does not compel us to be whole? Once again we can see how our freedom to choose becomes part of the picture. There are laws of health and laws of disease just as there are laws of good and evil, and, although God desires for us to choose the laws of health, he does not compel us to make those choices.

Much of our illness can be attributed directly to the choices we make. God does not compel us to eat too much, sleep too little, or mistreat our bodies. Nor does God compel us to eat the wrong foods, to forgo necessary exercise and care of one's body. These are choices we all can make without any help from God. Why, then, having made our choices, should we come back to him demanding, "How could you let this happen to me?"

Of course, not only do *our* choices impinge upon our health and well-being, but so do those of others. I may be injured just as easily by the carelessness of my neighbor's driving as I am by my own. If a neighbor allows unsanitary conditions to prevail in his yard, the health of my whole family may be affected by the choice that neighbor makes. My health may be jeopardized by the careless food packer, the indifferent manufacturer of drugs, the unrepentant polluter of our air and water. God does not will for any of these things to occur, but he allows me and all others to make these choices if that is what we want to do.

Furthermore, the choices we make as a society and as a nation may also affect our health. If as a nation we choose to spend billions of dollars for warfare instead of scientific research into cancer, for example, that is our choice to make. God does not compel us to use our material resources wisely. Yet these choices affect the health of billions of people.

31

It is true, too, that God allows us to be ignorant, if we want to be. He does not compel us to advance medical science or to institute programs of aid and assistance for the sick. If we want to continue in our present state of knowledge and helpfulness to one another, that is a decision we may make collectively.

The key, then, is our ability to make our own choices either in concert with his will or in defiance or ignorance of that will. As Emily Gardner Neal puts it: "That God *wills* disease, is to me, unthinkable. That he *permits* it is self-evident." [4]

Yet, even as we accept that proposition, we begin to try to think of exceptions to it. What about the child who is born with a congenital defect? Where is free will there? One answer, of course, is that birth defects are sometimes caused by prenatal diet, nutrition, health habits, as well as accidents. We need only remember the relatively large number of children born with birth defects that were later attributed to a certain drug given to the pregnant mothers.

Still, there seem to be some diseases that are not attributable to human free will. How do we explain these and still maintain that God's will is wholeness?

There were many times that I struggled with that question. Then, one day, a chance remark by a physician indicated a possible answer. He was describing the behavior of cancer cells. "They are cells," he said, "that have gone haywire, that have kicked over the traces and begun to do the very opposite of what they are supposed to do!"

The way he spoke of cancer cells made them sound like willful children who are rebelling against a parent. I began to wonder whether the principle of free will might be applicable to cells and organs as well as to human beings.

It wasn't long before I was finding that this idea was not the untrodden path that I had assumed it to be. Others had been there before me. Reading Paul Tournier's *The Meaning of Persons,* I was gratified to find him saying:

> Dr. Jean de Rougemont shows this [purposive expression] to be
> true even of the smallest cell of the organism: it chooses from its

surroundings what it is able to assimilate, and what serves to maintain life, and refuses the rest. . . . "It thus makes a choice. . . . In this constant selection there is clearly an element of memory and also of intelligence." [5]

Not memory, intelligence, or will on the level of self-conscious humanity to be sure, but at least the primitive prototypes of these. This was also the view of Teilhard de Chardin, the Roman Catholic cleric, paleontologist, and theologian. Teilhard looked at the natural world from the perspectives of both faith and science and saw in even the lowest organisms a " 'within,' a rudimentary responsiveness or sensitivity which is the forerunner of man's mental life." [6]

As human beings themselves are purposefully created, then, may we not also contend that cells and other organisms are created by God for a specific purpose or complex of functions? It is that design that we may designate as his "will" for these tiny items of creation; yet, even these tiny forms of life can "kick over the traces" and rebel against their design—and, in a sense, their Designer.

Evil, sickness, and tragedy seem high prices to pay for our free will; yet few of us would want to exchange our freedom for that kind of mechanical certainty. When once we know and accept the cost of something, we can find a way and means of living with that reality.

This recognition in relation to God's will not only provides us with a working answer but also deeply affects the way we go about dealing with God. If we are praying for healing, our task is not that of persuading a reluctant God to see things our way, nor a sleeping God to wake up and help us out. Many of our prayers and attempts at seeking God's help seem to reflect that kind of attitude—finding some way to get God to do our will.

If, however, we begin with the assumption that God wills for us to be whole and that in fact his desire for our healing is even greater than our own, then our approach in prayer is not so much a matter of striving as it is of yielding. Instead of trying to get across to God what we want him to do for us, we will concentrate more on putting ourselves in his hands so that he may do with us as he wills. My prayer, thus, will not be a matter of clenching my fists and trying to take heaven by storm, but, as Harry Emerson Fosdick put it, of "laying hold of God's highest willingness." And, instead of attempting to dam up the stream of his grace so that I may divert it to flow over my little project, I will, rather, endeavor to put myself gently within that stream of grace so that it may carry me to the destination that he has willed for me and all his children—the wholeness of mind, body, and spirit.

CHAPTER 4

Healing Is Not Magic

The space occupied at any given moment by electrons is less than a billionth part of the most solid object perceived by our senses so that the "material" part of our body could be contained in as little space as occupied by a droplet of water. Not only is the solidity of the body an illusion, but also the theory that the electronic pattern behind it is maintained by rigid laws of nature. Careful observation of individual atoms has proved that the electrons composing them behave in a completely unpredictable manner. In large numbers of atoms only do we find the regularities which have impressed physicists until the beginning of the present century as immutable laws of nature. A philosophy of absolute fatalism developed on the basis of these regularities, until physicists discovered that they were of a statistical nature.

———*Gotthard Booth, "Science and Spiritual Healing," in* Religion and Health

Recently on a daytime television talk show, two authorities on the subject of spiritual healing were interviewed by a well-known television newsman and personality. In the midst of a heated discussion on the validity of this approach to healing, the newsman exclaimed, "I could buy some of what you are saying if only there wasn't so much of the supernatural about it!"

This man is not alone in being turned off by the supernatural assumptions that many people suppose accompany the practice of spiritual healing. In the minds of these people, spiritual healing requires an intervention by God into the natural order, setting aside temporarily the laws of nature so that he may achieve his will over it. This is termed *supernatural,* meaning that it takes place outside or above the natural order.

Most of the people who believe in and practice a ministry of healing, however, do not regard it as supernatural at all. They may use instead the terms *supernormal* or *paranormal*. Both these terms imply that a phenomenon takes place according to some operation of the natural order of which we are either unaware or if aware, inadequately informed. Augustine said that "miracles do not happen in contradiction to nature, but only in contradiction to what is known of nature." A miracle, then, by this definition, is not supernatural (contrary to nature) but supernormal (contrary to what we know or expect of nature). Spiritual healing, thus, does not take place outside the laws of nature but within the natural order, about which, at this time, we know very little.

Just because we do not understand very much about the laws through which healing takes place does not mean that we must therefore reject the possibility that those laws exist. Today an increasing number of physicians are using effectively the ancient Chinese art of acupuncture. Five years ago it was relatively unknown to the medical profession in this country and to the public at large. When mentioned at all, it was linked with other seemingly occult subjects, such as astrology, palmistry, handwriting analysis, and the like. Today, for the most part, we still do not know what it is or how it works; yet our ignorance of these laws does not prevent us from using it effectively to alleviate human suffering. Furthermore, we often apply this same pragmatic approach to many areas of life.

All the practitioners of spiritual healing that I know believe that it is a law-abiding phenomenon. Some parapsychologists are conducting research in an attempt to discover the laws by which spiritual healing operates. We do not have to wait until we discover and comprehend those laws, however, to begin to use spiritual healing to bring wholeness to people in need of it.

Consider an oversimplified but instructive illustration. One hundred years ago not many people believed in the possibility of human flight. Flight by humans was rejected because it seemed that scientific evidence was clearly against the possibility of such a phenomenon. Two known forces made it "impossible" for man to fly through the air. First, there was gravity which would pull winged man back to earth—and in short order at that.

Furthermore, there was a force called *drag,* a force that prevents an object from sailing unimpeded through the atmosphere.

Because of these two scientific principles, human flight seemed utterly impossible. Today, however, we not only believe human flight is possible (if not frequently advisable), but people are daily flying in aircraft from one corner of the map to another. Now, if the forces of gravity and drag were valid barriers a century ago, what has happened to those barriers in the meantime?

The answer, of course, is obvious: scientific knowledge has progressed since then, and what was seemingly impossible according to what we knew a century ago is now an accepted reality on the basis of what we know today. In addition to the force of gravity, we have discovered and learned to utilize the force of *lift,* which creates an effect opposite that of gravity. In addition to the force of drag, we have learned how to apply the force of *thrust* which creates an effect quite opposite that of drag.

Because that which was once a dark corner of science has been explored and illuminated, we now can do what science would have persuaded us was quite impossible. Does this mean that these two counteractive forces, lift and thrust, have been devised only in the last one hundred years? No, these forces existed from the beginning of the world itself, but it has taken us this long to discover and utilize them. Yesterday's impossibilities become today's commonplace experiences.

Some years ago Dr. Sidney Burwell addressed the entering class of Harvard Medical School. At one point he observed:

> Gentlemen, in the next four years, here at school, we will teach you as much as we possibly can of the latest theories and interpretations of disease and all of its varieties and insidious forms. But medical science is progressing so rapidly that by the time you will have finished your four-year course, one-half of what we tell you will have been by that time proven incorrect and, unfortunately, we cannot tell you which half it's going to be.

Scientific knowledge in general and medical science in particular are constantly in a state of flux and change. Almost daily, medical "certainties" are being either discarded or revised

37

as we learn more and more about the natural order of the world in which God has placed us.

In spiritual healing I have come to believe that whatever happens when healing takes place in the human mind, body, or spirit is according to natural law within the order created by God. It is a miracle to us because we do not understand it and because it speaks to us of God's love and power. But it is not magic.

When a cleric places his hands on the head of a man kneeling at an altar railing during a healing service, when a mother holds and comforts her sick infant as she prays for him, when a little prayer circle lifts up intercessory prayers for someone hundreds of miles away, some of God's created natural laws are at work.

To some people, however, this denigrates God's role in human affairs. The reason for this misconception is often a rather inadequate understanding of how God works in the world. Many people think of God and his world like this:

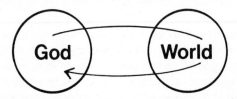

In this scheme of things, God is outside the world occasionally, either at our invitation or at his own caprice, reaching into the world, setting aside the laws that usually govern it, and accomplishing some "unnatural" goal (like a healing). This means that God intervenes in the world from time to time.

Perhaps, however, it would help us to think of God and his world in this manner:

This diagram places God within the world he has created. The diagram does not mean to infer that he is limited to this world or is identical with it. If God, then, is not "out there" somewhere but is here in the world, then we do not have to call upon God to stop the world in order that he may perform a miracle for us. The natural order does not need to be suspended or sent on vacation; it continues to operate as always. God does not need to intervene in the world because he is already in it.

Thus, God does not need to be relegated to the emergency squad. He is in the world working in many different ways to accomplish his will. When a wound heals in the human body, God is in that healing process. If a drug is administered by a physician to help a patient toward recovery, God is in that prescription. If a surgeon operates to remove a diseased organ, God is in the surgery, both in the skill of the surgeon's hands and in the surgical knowledge inspired by his Spirit. And if a deeply concerned person lifts up prayers of intercession for another person who is ill, God is in those prayers, in the love that inspired them, and in the natural forces those prayers call into action.

For some people there is a stumbling block in thinking that God works in this world, not through sanctified magic, but through the natural forces that he created and set into motion. In their eyes, this seems to downgrade the activity of the Divine Being. That view, however, is neither necessary nor biblical. The writer of the creation stories in Genesis, for example, saw nothing second-rate about the natural order God created. "And God saw everything that he had made, and behold, it was very good" (Gen. 1:31).

For God to use the natural order that he created so that he might accomplish his redemptive purpose for mankind is no less impressive than if he used a supernatural bag of tricks to override the world he created. God's natural order is a thing of beauty and wonder all by itself. It was this sense of wonder at the created world that led Roman Catholic priest and paleontologist Teilhard de Chardin to exclaim:

Lord God, my dignity as a man forbids me to shut my eyes to this, like an animal or a child; therefore lest I succumb to the temptation to curse the universe, *teach me to adore it by seeing you hidden within it*. Say once again to me, Lord, those great and liberating words, the words which are at once revealing light and effective power: *hoc est Corpus meum* ["This is my Body"].[1]

Before we leave this subject, it is important also that we realize that the term *natural laws* is only a tool for understanding the ways in which the world works. Perhaps we have trouble with the concept of God working in his world because our concept of natural laws is too rigid, because we have taken this term too literally.

What we call, for want of a better term, the laws of nature are actually not laws at all. One writer, Henry Bett, has termed them "nothing more than statements of regularity, constructed by our minds, and imposed on nature."[2] There is, of course, a God-created natural order, but it is not identical with the body of natural laws that we know today. Our understanding of the natural order of our world is but an interpretation of a much more complex, mind-boggling reality.

When I first became interested in the ministry of spiritual healing, I made a rather startling personal discovery: I possessed a very fine nineteenth-century scientific mind! The problem with that, of course, is that we do not live in the nineteenth century but the twentieth, and a nineteenth-century mind, however fine, is not adequate for the world in which we live today.

My scientific world view held the universe as a gigantic machine. That machine, once set in motion, operated with a kind of comforting, although boring, regularity. It went nowhere and admitted to nothing new under the sun. There was no room in that great machine for purpose (except to keep doing the same thing over and over again) or for progress.

I have come to realize that the world is not a machine at all. If we must compare it to anything, let us liken it to an organism, a living, growing, developing thing. My world had been pre-evolutionary in outlook, and I was challenged to see this world as having a goal, a purpose, a direction, a growth, a development, or an evolution. I have come to see this world God created as a place

40

in which, by his grace, a new thing can happen. All kinds of mutations can occur in a living, dynamic world that is constantly growing and developing.

I no longer view God, then, as an absentee landlord who got it all started a long time ago and comes around periodically to collect the rent or to make a few necessary repairs. I believe in a God who not only created but is still creating today. "My Father is working still, and I am working," said Jesus (John 5:17).

I do not see the natural order and the concept of natural law as a limiting perspective of the Divine Being but as one that allows us to see a bigger God in a bigger universe. Scientific determinism is no more attractive than theological determinism. As Henry Bett puts it:

> Whence comes the persistent fallacy, which haunts so many minds today, that the laws of nature are the explanation of events and even the cause of events? Obviously they are not, as every scientist and every logician of any eminence has repeatedly confessed. They are merely statements of the regular way in which things normally recur, when regarded from one particular point of view. . . .
>
> A natural law then is not a cause, and not an explanation: it is an abstract rule relating to the regular behavior of natural events.[3]

Several years ago, J. B. Philips wrote a book entitled *Your God Is Too Small*. He was quite correct. For many of us, our concept of both the Creator and his creation is too small, too limited, too parochial. The ministry of spiritual healing requires a bigger, greater God and a more complex, more wonderful universe than that to which many of us are accustomed.

CHAPTER 5

Healing the Whole Man

We have spent too much time criticizing healers because they are not doctors and not enough time criticizing doctors who are not healers.

—Jesuit Father Louis Beirnaent at the meeting of the International Congress of Parapsychology, St. Paul, France, May, 1954

Jerry Kramer, once a star performer with the Green Bay Packers football team, has compared the late coach Vince Lombardi to a spiritual healer:

Coach Lombardi never takes second place when it comes to Oral Roberts or any of the rest of the healers. He can just walk into a training room filled with football players, and he'll say, "What the hell's wrong with you guys? There's nobody in here hurt." And the dressing room will clear immediately. And all the wounded will be healed.[1]

Many will hastily ascribe Coach Lombardi's apparent powers of healing to the presumption that the players were faking their injuries or, at best, simply that they imagined they were hurt. We are coming to realize, however, that we must not jump to conclusions as to what is a real or an imagined illness or injury. In fact, the very meaning of the term *psychosomatic* indicates that such an illness is not all in the mind. The term is an acknowledgment that the mind and spirit *(psyche)* and the body *(soma)* are constantly interacting with each other.

There is a common tendency to assume that if the mind or emotions play a part in our illness, the malady is largely imaginary, not real. There is an illustrative story about a little girl who one day was stopped by a neighbor who asked, "How's everything at your house these days?" "Well," replied the little girl, "pretty good, except for Grandpa. He's been awful sick."

"Nonsense," protested her neighbor, "that's all in his mind. You tell him I said he just thinks he's sick." "OK," retorted the little girl uncertainly as she hurried on her way.

Several weeks later the two met again. "Well," beamed the neighbor confidently, "How's your Grandpa now? Does he still think he's sick?" "Oh, no," replied the little girl with great solemnity, "now he thinks he's dead; we buried him last week."

As a man "thinketh in his heart," said the writer of Proverbs, "so is he" (23:7 KJV). If a person thinks he is sick, that illness will not be confined to just his mind but will affect the body as well.

Much of our problem here is the failure to regard the patient as a whole being. In the hospital we may hear medical personnel refer to a patient as "the cardiac in room 301" or "the brain tumor down the hall." Of course, these may simply represent an institutional shorthand, but the impersonal overtones also suggest that there may be a preoccupation with malfunctioning organs rather than concern with whole persons.

When I was a boy the "germ theory" was the most popular explanation for sickness and disease. Simply stated, it went something like this: if you're sick, it's because you have a germ; and if you're not sick, it's because you are free of germs. I was made to be very concious of germs, and they were everywhere. I often felt like the little boy who exclaimed, "Jesus and germs! Jesus and germs! That's all I ever hear about, and I've never seen either of them!"

Well, I had never seen any germs, but I knew they were all about me, and I did my utmost to make sure that I protected myself from them lest they succeed in their diabolical plan to make me ill. I was absolutely horrified to see people who ate without washing their hands and did all kinds of unsanitary—and therefore dangerous—things.

Today, although I am no more fond of germs than I was as a child, I realize that germs are not the root cause of illness. When I allow myself to think about it, I realize that germs are all around me every minute of the day. The room in which I am sitting as I write these words, apparently quite clean, is nevertheless "crawling" with germs! So, if the world around us is so full of germs, why are we not sick all the time?

The answer, of course, is that the body has an immunizing system that, when it is functioning rightly, battles against the germs and sickness-producing agents and keeps them from taking over and making us ill. These battles are constantly being fought within us, for the most part without our ever knowing. We are told, for instance, that X rays indicate that many of us have had tuberculosis without ever knowing it. We know that because scar tissue shows up on X rays indicating that the battle took place and the disease lost. Dr. O. Carl Simonton, a cancer specialist in Fort Worth, Texas, tells us that many people have similarly had cancer without knowing it.

Thus, when the body is functioning the way God created it to, health is maintained. What, then, causes the body not to function as God intends? Very often the answer is that our emotional state or our spiritual condition may make the difference between sickness and disease. As somebody has put it, "It's not so much what kind of bug has the feller as what kind of feller has the bug."

Some physicians go as far as saying that all sickness is psychosomatic: caused by the interplay of mind and spirit with the body. Dr. Arnold Hutschnecker, for example, says:

> Illness is the outer expression of a deep and possibly dangerous struggle going on within. . . .
>   We are moving toward the recognition that in illness of any kind, from the common cold to cancer, emotional stress plays a part.[2]

Without becoming involved in the controversy between those who say that all sicknesses are psychosomatic and those who say only some are, we can at least agree that the interrelationship of mind, body, and spirit is a critical factor in understanding and treating disease. Furthermore, we can also understand why it is important to treat the whole person rather than just a malfunctioning organ. It is the person who is "dis-eased," not just a part of him. We need to deal with causes, not just treat symptoms.

Thousands of years ago, Socrates said, "The reason for the frequent failure of the Greek doctors is their inadequate knowledge of the whole, the health of which is a necessary condition of that of the part." [3]

Is not this likely the reason that so many people "doctor" for so many years, progressing from one chronic ailment to another or remaining with the same condition or set of conditions year after year? The physician may be intelligently and skillfully treating the symptoms yet never penetrating to the cause that may lie quite beyond his competence or training. He is treating only a part of the person, but, as Italian psychiatrist Emilio Servadio puts it, "Healing consists of a readjustment of the patient's whole personality." [4]

Causality, we must remember, is often quite complex, regardless how simplistically we approach most of the phenomena of life. For the sake of illustration, let us assume a hypothetical case: a middle-aged man, let's call him Sam, suffers from emphysema, a disease of the lungs that impairs a person's capacity for proper breathing.

Sam consults his family physician who ascribes the causation of the disease to Sam's excessive smoking of cigarettes. "I've told you a hundred times to cut down or something like this would happen," he tells the wheezing Sam.

Sam is not entirely satisfied with that diagnosis, however, mainly because he doesn't want to give up smoking. So, because he has good hospitalization insurance, he has himself admitted to a local hospital for a battery of tests. After considerable time and expense he is informed that his problem is a congenital condition, something he inherited with his genes.

Despite the time and money spent on the diagnosis, however, the condition continues to worsen. At last, Sam is persuaded to see a psychiatrist. After many sessions, the therapist and the patient come to the conclusion that his problem is caused by a deep-seated guilt complex. He is apparently punishing himself in an unconscious manner.

That sounds good, but the condition doesn't improve, and so

Sam casts about for whatever answers he can find. An environmentalist assures him that the problem is the consequence of heavy air pollution in Sam's part of town. A nutritionist tells him that he lacks the proper amounts of magnesium in his diet. A friend sends him to a chiropractor who finds a pinched nerve as the culprit. The neighbors discount all these solutions, for they have observed Sam and his family over the years, and they are convinced that Sam's condition is primarily his unconscious response to a nagging wife and daughter. His emphysema is the only means whereby poor Sam can get any relief and sympathy in the household. Other friends send Sam to a spiritualist who tells Sam that he is under "spirit attack," and to a reincarnationist who assures Sam that the emphysema is his karma and that he had better just learn to live with it.

Now, which of these has put their finger on the cause of Sam's affliction?

But why must it be just *the* cause, a single factor? Why not a complex of causitive factors that have converged upon Sam over a period of time? Quite likely Sam does smoke too much. Perhaps he is suffering from a guilt complex. Perhaps even he lacks sufficient magnesium in his diet, suffers from air pollution and a pinched nerve in his back, and perhaps it is a nagging household that makes escape in emphysema a lesser evil. Sam is a complex person, and his physical condition is likely a manifestation of a number of things that are disharmonious in his life.

The Chicago Institute for Psychoanalysis has conducted a ten-year study of seven diseases to determine their psychosomatic relationships. Their findings indicate the following:

Duodenal ulcer patients—persons who experience frustration of their dependency needs for love and comfort

Ulcerative colitis patients—persons who have lost hope of accomplishing a task that involves responsibility, effort, and concentration

Bronchial asthma patients—persons who have been threatened with the loss of a mother or a mother-substitute attachment. "Asthma attacks are explained as an inhibited use of the respiratory tract for communication, a substitute for crying or confession. The common allergic disease, hay fever, is a minor form of asthma.''

Hypertension (high blood pressure) patients—people who have been engaged in a continuous struggle against expressing their hostile-agressive feelings, with a consequent difficulty in asserting themselves

Neurodermatitis (skin disorders ascribed to "nerves") patients—persons who feel a conflict between their exhibitionism, guilt, and masochism, combined with strong needs for the physical expression of love from others

Arthritis patients—persons who experience great difficulty in handling aggressive-hostile impulses, but differ from hypertensive patients in combining self-control with a benevolent tyranny over others. (''The typical mother of the arthritic patient is said to have been a restrictive one.'' The disease is frequently precipitated ''when a husband or child makes a successful attempt to stand up to the domination.'')

Thyrotoxiscosis (over-functioning of the thyroid gland) patients—persons who live in a constant struggle against fear, often manifested specifically as a fear of death[5]

Once again we must be careful not to respond to this kind of data in a simplistic manner. We must not assume that these personality characteristics are the only contexts from which these diseases can develop, nor must we assume that some simple changes in the personality will quickly change the condition. For example, it is believed by some physicians that the psychic origin of the allergy we call hay fever is a suppressed desire to cry. This does not mean, however, that crying will cure this malady. What it means is that, understanding something of its genesis, we can begin the process of reconditioning the personality and end the conditioned response of illness that has continued well beyond the need it was originally intended to meet.

Some physicians have found that an emotional trauma six to

eight months before the onset of the disease is typical of cancer patients. Dr. O. Carl Simonton has found that patients often make a better response to therapy when they have been put in touch with that emotional trauma, identifying it and understanding it.[6]

A wholistic approach is important, not only in understanding the origin of the disease, but also in applying therapy for its cure. A past president of the American Cancer Society, E. P. Pendregrass, has stated that there is substantial evidence to indicate that the course of cancer is often affected by emotional distress.[7] Another authority, Dr. Bruno Klopfer, former president of the Society for Projective Techniques, in an address, "Psychological Variables in Human Cancer," tells of his success in using patients' Rorschach tests in order to predict whether their cancer was a fast-growing or slow-growing malignancy. The rationale of his experiments is predicated on "a symbiotic relationship between the patient and his cancer." Dr. Klopfer goes on to explain:

> If a good deal of the vital energy that the patient has at his disposal is used up in the defense of an insecure ego, then the organism seems not to have the vital energy at his disposal to fight the cancer off and the cancer has easy going. If, however, a minimum of vital energy is consumed in ego defensiveness, then the cancer has a hard time making headway.[8]

Dr. Klopfer uses psychological terminology—*insecure ego* and *ego defensiveness*—but we may just as easily translate these terms into a religious vernacular: faith, hope, guilt, despair, and so on.

The wholistic approach to illness and disease is necessary for both the physician and the religionist. Writing on "Body, Mind, and Spirit," Dr. John A. P. Millet, a physician, acknowledges:

> Modern medical practice at the best level takes full cognizance of the fact that the human being must be considered as a total entity, not just as someone who has a bad pair of tonsils, a grumbling appendix, or a low basal metabolism. . . .
>   The significance of the illness to the patient, the pressures under which he has lived, the attitudes of those nearest him, his economic and social situation, and the outstanding traits in his personality—all these, and perhaps other special factors must be

evaluated, and their contribution to the total picture of disability must be correctly estimated. If this is not done the adrenalin may check the asthma, the ointment relieve the eczema, and the diet heal the ulcer, but the whole patient is little altered and the same break in his adaptive efficiency may well occur again. . . .

Medical science, therefore, has reluctantly consented to abandon the simpler task of investigating the human organism as a mechanic examines an automobile which breaks down on a highway.[9]

Thus, it is not a question of whether the patient should seek medical *or* spiritual therapy but of realizing that in every illness there are both medical *and* spiritual perspectives, and healing is likely to be more efficacious when medicine and religion are willing to work hand in hand. As medicine pursues the complexities of psychosomatic medicine, the church must rediscover its almost forgotten role and responsibility in a ministry of spiritual healing.

CHAPTER 6

Many Channels, One Healer

Theology and medicine lost the intimate connection they originally had, and always should have—for saving the person is healing him. The tremendous importance which the healing stories have in the New Testament records is understandable only if one knows that the Kingdom of God was supposed to come as the healing power on earth. But the church, although reading one of these stories in almost every Sunday service, did not emphasize their healing side. . . . The rapproachment between theology and medicine in our time has brought a great liberation to such men by opening a new way for preaching about the healing stories in the New Testament.

——Paul Tillich, "The Impact of Psychotherapy on Theological Thought," in The Churches' Handbook for Spiritual Healing

Bruce Larson, whose name for many years has been identified with the Faith at Work movement, tells of becoming suddenly ill at a religious conference in Bloomington, Illinois. His symptoms seemed to be those of influenza, and he felt so bad that he was put to bed in the men's dormitory. Within one hour's time, six different people had heard of his plight and came to do for him what they could.

The first of these came with oil and anointed him with it for healing. The second person knelt by his bed and said a prayer of intercession. The third, a doctor, took his pulse, gave him some aspirin, and assured him that it was probably the twenty-four-hour flu bug. The next person brought him a tray of food which, at the time, seemed the least likely thing he would want. A fifth person came, talked with him briefly, and expressed concern. But the most fascinating of all was the sixth, a Finnish masseuse, who gave him a massage and sang hymns in Finnish.

The outcome of these diverse therapies: Larson says, "I was healed within the hour. I don't know which of these people was the channel of God's healing, but I suspect they were all used." [1]

I would go a step further and change Larson's suspicion to an affirmation: God uses many different channels to accomplish his healing will. There is but one Healer behind a multitude of healing arts and ministries. Thus, although I may speak of the ministry of healing, it is a multifaceted unity of many ministries, diverse approaches, methods, and dynamics.

Writing on "Spiritual Healing in the Light of History," church historian Cyril Richardson distinguishes between two different types of spiritual healing. The first of these he designates "*charismatic* healing, where the healer himself plays the primary role." [2] This is a person who is specially gifted along the lines of which the apostle Paul is speaking in I Corinthians 12. Included in this category would be people like Olga Worrall and Ethel DeLoach in the United States, the late Harry Edwards and Gordon Turner in England, to name just a few. Each of these persons is recognized as a healer. (Although they are called "healers," each would be quick to point out that God alone is the Healer and to say, "I am simply a channel through whom God works.")

Professor Richardson indicates another type of healing which he delineates as "sacramental" healing. This type of healing, he says, "depends for its efficiency upon the power of religious tradition and the faith of the Church." In this case, it is not "the charismatic individual, but the sacramental form [which] is of primary importance." [3] In this type of healing we are dependent upon the gift given to the church rather than to an individual. Simply to *be* the church means to bear the gift of healing (as well as other spiritual gifts).

The distinction Professor Richardson draws is helpful in understanding the diversity of the healing ministry, but the two types of healing that he indicates are not mutually exclusive. In fact, some ministries of healing utilize what he terms "charismatic" and "sacramental" healing. For example, a pastor may be specially gifted as a healer and may conduct a ministry of healing that is also sacramental. This was true of Dr. Alfred Price, for many years the rector of St. Stephen's Episcopal Church in Philadelphia and warden of the International Order of St. Luke the Physician, an interdenominational organization founded to promote the ministry of healing in the church. His internationally known ministry combined both the charismatic and sacramental perspectives. It is true also of the combined ministry of Dr. Olga Worrall, a much-tested lay healer, and Dr. Robert Kirkley, a United Methodist minister, at the New Life Clinic of the Mount Washington United Methodist Church in Baltimore. Both are charismatically gifted and together pursue a ministry that is also sacramental.

The term *specially gifted* must be understood as a relative one. I believe that all persons possess a gift of healing to some degree. A number of years ago, the producer of a national network television show asked me to go to New York to consult with his staff concerning a possible TV program that would be devoted to spiritual healing. After approximately an hour of consultation in their New York studio, one of the staff members asked casually, "You don't believe everyone has this gift, do you?" "Yes, I do," I replied, "although not to the same degree." I went on to liken the distribution of the gift of healing to the distribution of musical ability. Some people are gifted with musical genius, others have the ability to be topflight professionals, still others to be talented amateurs, while others have a rather modest gift that could probably be cultivated and improved. My experience in giving voice training to supposedly tone-deaf people convinced me that even the slightest amount of endowment can be developed to some degree.

The television man listened patiently, but when I was finished he asked, "Well, but you wouldn't say that on the air, would you?" Admittedly nonplussed, I said that I would if I were asked. "But if we asked you not to say that on the air, you wouldn't? You see, people are not too likely to be interested in watching a program about a gift that everyone has." Once again I replied that that was what I would answer if I were asked. After an awkward pause, the producer stood up to signify the end of the interview and said, "OK, we'll be in touch with you." They never did contact me, and I understand that after several more preliminary interviews with healers, they decided not to have the program.

I still believe that everyone may have the gift of healing to a varying degree. There are people who are specially gifted and who have an amazing track record in their ministry. Still there are times when a member of the family or a friend may be more helpful to us as channels of healing. We may not seem to have much of the gift of healing, but sometimes when we offer God what we have he is able to magnify greatly that offering for his purposes. It is not unusual to hear a mother say that she has given healing to her child. And there have been times when I have heard of a child who was instrumental in bringing healing to a parent or other member of the family.

The late Gordon Turner, a brilliant British healer, defines spiritual healing as including "all forms of therapeutics that are directed at removing disease through the stimulation of a spiritual process." [4] Thus defined, we may see spiritual healing operate in many different ways:

through *the laying on of hands:*	a. by a pastor or lay healer in a worship service
	b. by a healer operating in a home, clinic, or hospital
through *intercessory prayer:*	a. by a charismatic healer
	b. by a healer in a church service
	c. by a prayer group
	d. by a concerned person
through *anointing with oil:*	a. in a church service
	b. in hospital or home
through *petitionary prayer:*	a. in a worship service
	b. in a special healing service
	c. in home or hospital
through *counseling:*	a. by a pastor/healer
	b. by a concerned friend
	c. by a professional counselor

The listings above are not meant to be exhaustive but to represent, rather, the many diverse methods, styles, and settings for healing. A church may have a weekly healing service, or it may be periodic. (One church I know of has a healing service monthly; another, four or five times per year.) The church may include a special period for healing prayer in its usual Sunday service, or only on occasions of special need. The ministry may be carried on by an individual, by a group, or by the whole church. Some healers use anointing with oil on a regular basis; others use it only when requested or when it seems to have special significance. Some churches combine the celebration of Holy Communion with the healing service. Sometimes the healing is part of a charismatic service or meeting, combined with glossolalia (speaking in tongues).

This same diversity is seen in the practice of laying on hands. Some healers merely place their hands lightly upon the head of the patient. Others will place their hands on parts of the body that are significantly affected by the disease. Some do not touch the patient at all, preferring to hold their hands several inches from the patient's body, either in a stationary position or in undulating movements around the body. (Ethel DeLoach uses this approach, and her method of healing seems to be significantly related to the acupuncture points of the body.) Some healers place their hands upon the patient for a standard period of time, giving each patient the same amount of time, while other healers vary the length of treatment as they seem to be "led." Some healers, like the Presbyterian healer the Rev. Alex Holmes, combine laying on of hands with the manipulation of limbs. Still others may sometimes combine it with chiropractic or osteopathic "adjustments."

Some healers have no contact with the patient except through the laying on of hands or a prayer request. Others will spend considerable time in counseling with the patient, exploring spiritual dimensions of the problem, and prescribing spiritual therapies. Some healers prescribe a type of meditation as both a preparation for healing and a healing technique in itself (see chapter 13). Some healers doing "absent healing" require only the name of the patient, while others ask for information about the illness or problem and often a photograph. Many healing ministries ask for no remuneration—and some steadfastly refuse to accept anything—while some will accept donations, and others for whom healing has become a vocation even designate a fee.

Some healers use color and music in their therapies. Two that I know of—the late Edgar Cayce, and Ross Peterson—go into a kind of "trance state" and do both diagnosis and prescription without the benefit of medical knowledge. The late Kathryn Kuhlman often found that people were healed where they sat in the auditorium before they were brought to her on the stage or platform. At Lourdes there are verified medical records of healings that have taken place as people have knelt at the shrine or received the waters of that revered spring. Some healers work in an emotionally charged atmosphere (Kathryn Kuhlman and Oral Roberts both used to work in this manner), while other healers, such as Gordon Turner, eschewed the use of emotion.

Although Episcopalians and United Methodists often seem to be more frequently involved in the spiritual healing movements, this ministry represents a wide diversity of backgrounds. Kathryn Kuhlman was a Pentacostal. Oral Roberts is now a United Methodist but began his ministry in a Pentacostal background. Olga Worrall is Russian Orthodox, although her whole ministry has been focused in two United Methodist churches. As I have indicated, the Rev. Alex Holmes is a Presbyterian, as is medical doctor Clair B. King of Canton, Ohio. As previously noted, Dr. Alfred Price is an Episcopalian; so are lay healer Emily Gardner Neal and Dr. John Ellis Large. Father Francis MacNutt is Roman Catholic, Harry Edwards was a British spiritualist, and Gordon Turner, a deeply spiritual person although basically nonsectarian.

(There are other seemingly gifted healers who are not within the Christian tradition, but this study will focus on those who are. It is important for us to realize, however, that the gift of healing is not limited by doctrinal and ecclesiastical considerations.)

What all these diverse ministries and healers have in common is the conviction that God alone is the healer and that they are but channels that he in some way uses to achieve his healing purpose. Most of these would also agree that their gift or ministry is dependent, not upon a supernatural power but a supernormal or paranormal force mediated by God. As Professor Cyril Richardson puts it, they find it "no more 'natural' for a disease to pursue its usual course, than for it to eventuate in spontaneous healing. The difference lies in the kind of natural powers that are brought to bear on the situation." [5]

Not only is it necessary to see this diversity of healing ministries and methods in a wholistic perspective but all healing arts and sciences as well. The concept of spiritual healing sees all medical healing within this same context. Medical healing uses different therapies, but we believe that the Source is still the same, and there is still but one Healer. Many doctors would agree with the oft quoted physician who said, "I set the bone, but God does the healing."

Sometimes people will assume that if they have faith in God, they need not see a physician. I was asked to visit a parishioner's friend in the hospital. She was suffering from a dangerous kidney disease, and her physicians were talking about a kidney transplant, which frightened her terribly. "Pastor, please pray for me so that I won't have to go through a transplant," she asked desperately. "Isn't it true that if I have enough faith, I won't need it?" "Not necessarily," was my surprising reply. "Mary," I continued, "did you ever stop to think that God uses many different means to accomplish his purpose? I truly believe he wants you well, but I'm not about to tell him how he must accomplish his own purpose."

Mary looked very doubtful, but I continued. "It may well be that God intends to heal you through the kidney transplant. That also takes faith, you know." Mary sank back against her pillow and was silent for what seemed a very long time. Finally, she looked at me and said quietly, "OK, I'll try. Would you pray for me as you think best?"

As I prayed I had the feeling that if Mary could let go and permit God to use whatever means he wanted to use, she might not need the kidney transplant. Her willingness to commit herself to God's love might be the key to her healing. I said nothing of this to her, and when I left the room I was unsure of what direction her faith was taking.

Several days later she called me on the telephone. Her voice was ecstatic: "I don't have to have the operation, and the doctor says I can go home tomorrow!" I cannot know what were the dynamics that produced that happy result, but I am convinced that Mary experienced healing because she came to realize that God heals in many different ways and through many different people.

With its consistent emphasis on wholeness, the ministry of spiritual healing may serve to help bring all the healing arts and sciences together in mutual recognition that God heals through the family doctor, the specialist, the surgeon, the dentist, the pharmacist, the nutritionist, the psychiatrist, the chiropractor, the physical therapist, the school counselor, the pastor, the healer, the prayer group, and the concerned neighbor or loved one.

I look forward to the day when the general practitioner may refer the patient to an osteopathic physician, when the dentist may recommend the patient to a psychiatrist, when the surgeon may recommend a spiritual healer, and the dermatologist a visit to the pastor's study.

That day may not be as far off as it may seem. I find many physicians who are more concerned to make people whole than to protect a medically parochial point of view. I know not a few physicians who are willing to follow truth wherever it may lead—even into a rival practitioner's office. On a number of occasions physicians have asked me to work with their patients, using spiritual healing methods. One doctor called me late at night to come quickly to administer healing to his wife whose condition had resisted all medical therapies.

The ministry of healing must not be cut off from the practice of medicine, and the medical practitioner must not cut himself off from knowledge of spiritual therapies. Medicine and religion, physician and spiritual healer, can work hand in hand acknowledging that there are many therapies but just one Healer.

CHAPTER 7

Healing in the Laboratory

I'm skared. Lots of people who work at the collidge and the pepul at the medicil school came to wish me luk. I hope I have luk. I got my rabits foot and my luky penny and my horshoe. I dont no what science is but they all keep saying it so maybe its something that helps you have good luk.

—*Daniel Keyes*, Flowers for Algernon

Several years ago while I was speaking to a group in Charlotte, North Carolina, on the subject of healing, a physician present mentioned a new book by a Dr. Nolen that was reported to "thoroughly document that spiritual healing is quite lacking in any validity whatsoever." Had I read this book, he wanted to know, and, if I had, what was my response to it. My answer was that I had not read it but would do so as soon as possible.

Soon afterward I read a review of *Healing: A Doctor in Search of a Miracle* by William A. Nolen, M.D. The review hailed the book and exclaimed, "At last: scientific proof to dispel once and for all the 'healing' quackery!"

I had hoped to borrow the book or perhaps to wait for it to appear in paperback, but the review persuaded me that I couldn't wait for either. Upon reading it, I found that Dr. Nolen, who is a syndicated newspaper columnist as well as a small-town surgeon, had begun his investigation "in the hope of finding a true healer" but quickly concluded:

> Two years ago I began looking for a healing miracle. When I started my search I hoped to find some evidence that someone, somewhere, had supernatural powers that he or she could employ to cure those patients we doctors, with all our knowledge and training, must still label "incurable." As I have said before, I have been unable to find any such miracle worker.[1]

Dr. Nolen's research, it developed, would hardly have been adequate for a college freshman's term paper. It consisted of one solitary visit to a Kathryn Kuhlman healing service, a clumsy follow-up on some of the people allegedly cured at that service, a visit to a reputed healer in Houston, and a trip to the Philippines to view the so-called psychic surgeons who are hardly, if at all, in the mainstream of the ministry of spiritual healing. That was the extent of his "research." Although he apparently knew of Allen Spraggett's excellent study of Kathryn Kuhlman, *Kathryn Kuhlman: The Woman Who Believes in Miracles*—he uses it to speculate on the healer's age—he makes no reference at all to Spraggett's evidential case studies in that book, case studies that would have significantly challenged Dr. Nolen's hasty conclusions. Nolen's book, which might have been more appropriately entitled *Healing: A Doctor in Search of a Best Seller,* contains no bibliography, no appendix, and only one footnote. It makes no reference at all to some of the various types of research that are being pursued in this field. Despite Dr. Nolen's book's pretensions, it is not scientific research. I am in favor of scientific research into spiritual healing; unfortunately Dr. Nolen's book is not that, not by the greatest stretch of the imagination.

As to the research that Dr. Nolen's book ignored, it is not yet conclusive, but it has provided some substantial evidence for the validity of spiritual healing. Since this book is intended for a more general readership and not the technician and because more detailed and statistically supported descriptions of most of these experiments have been reported elsewhere, I will simply try to describe each of these areas of research and the findings and indicate in the chapter notes where the reader may turn for a more technical and documented treatment.

Among the best-known efforts have been those of Dr. Bernard Grad of McGill University in Montreal. Aware of the customary rebuttal that supposed healings of people were the result of psychological manipulation, suggestion, or the hysterical relief of psychosomatic symptoms, Dr. Grad studied the healing effect of the hands of reputed healer Colonel Oskar Estebany upon mice that had been surgically wounded. Using two groups under identical conditions, one group to be treated by Colonel Estebany's hands, the other to serve as a control group without treatment, Dr. Grad found statistically significant evidence that the mice treated by Colonel Estebany healed more rapidly.[2]

In a second set of experiments designed to limit even further the possible uncontrolled effects of physical handling, Dr. Grad had the healer treat vials of water that were then used to water "wounded" seeds. Again there was an untreated control group, and Dr. Grad found significant statistical evidence that the seeds watered with the treated solution were more likely to sprout, grow faster, and produce plants that weighed more.[3]

Another set of well-known experiments was carried on by Sister M. Justa Smith, a Roman Catholic nun with a doctorate in biochemistry, whose special field of competence is enzymes (believed by some to be the catlytic agents in the body's ability to heal itself). She also used Colonel Estebany and found that his treatment of enzymes in vials brought statistically significant results. In further experiments with other healers, particularly Olga Worrall, Dr. Smith used three different kinds of enzymes: trypsin, which she had used in her first experiments; NAD (nicotinomide-diuncleotide); and amylase-amylose.

To promote healing, each of these enzymes needs to react in a different manner: trypsin needs to be accelerated in its activity; NAD needs to be decelerated; and amylase-amylose needs to remain at the same level. Without telling the healers which enzyme they were treating or suggesting what kind of result was required (acceleration, deceleration, or maintainance of status quo), Dr. Smith found that each enzyme responded to the healing treatments in the optimum manner: trypsin accelerated, NAD decelerated, and amylase-amylose remained at the same level. One can hardly help concluding that there is in the healing power an "intelligence" that elicits from the healee's enzymes the response that is most propitious for health and wholeness.[4]

Less widely publicized were the experiments conducted by a number of British healers under the direction of the late Gordon

Turner. One set of experiments called for cut chrysanthemums. It was observed that a group of flowers that received healing stayed fresh considerably longer than the untreated control group. Furthermore, reported Neville Randall in the *London Daily Sketch,* when Gordon Turner passed his hands over the flowers to give them treatment, "their heads seemed to sway slightly following the movements he made." One group of chrysanthemums stayed fresh for fifty-five days!

Gordon Turner also conducted experiments with ordinary grass seed. After many repetitions of the experiment, Turner noted that the seeds that received healing were "never less than 3 days ahead of the sample which remained untreated." Furthermore, Turner found that "in every instance the treated sample was a deeper green." These experiments led Turner to muse that "it may well be that such old-fashioned rituals as 'blessing crops' have considerable substance in fact. Simple prayer might prove to be a far more efficacious 'fertiliser' than a great many expensive and dangerous chemicals." [5]

Some of Gordon Turner's experiments were with patients, although he found these experiments much harder to control in terms of variables and patient psychology. From these experiments with patients he concluded that both absent and contact (touch) healing "achieve a similar rate of success (possibly between 55%–70%)." [6]

Perhaps the most tested healer in the world today is Dr. Olga Worrall of Baltimore. In addition to the experiments conducted with her by Dr. M. Justa Smith, Dr. Worrall has also been tested by a number of other serious researchers, including Dr. Thelma Moss, U.C.L.A.; Dr. Robert N. Miller, a research scientist in the engineering-materials laboratory of the Lockheed-Georgia Company; and Dr. Edward Brame, a research chemist with DuPont in Wilmington, Delaware.

In one experiment, Mrs. Worrall "gave healing" to special samples of water. One sample of water was treated by Dr. Worrall, another by a different healer, and two were not treated. In testing the samples of water with a spectrometer, Dr. Brame found statistically significant differences in the molecular structure of the water samples treated by the healers. Subsequent heat-capacity tests by a colleague at the University of Delaware yielded similar findings.[7]

Another interesting and evidential test was conducted by Dr. Robert N. Miller using a cloud chamber. In this experiment a glass cylinder with an aluminum bottom and viewing glass at the top is used as a chamber in which a zone of alcohol mist is produced when alcohol is introduced into the chamber and the assembly is placed on a flat block of dry ice. If high-energy atomic particles pass through this sensitive zone, a path of vapor trails is generated.

In one portion of the experiment, Olga Worrall placed her hands around the cylinder as if it were a patient receiving treatment. It was soon evident that Dr. Worrall was producing a wave motion within the cloud chamber, apparently generated by her healing energy. Dr. Miller tells us that "several weeks later, from a distance of 600 miles, she caused a turbulence to develop within the chamber."[8]

Dr. Miller also conducted significant experiments with Dr. Worrall in which the effects of her healing energies upon the growth rate of rye grass was measured, this healing given from the distance of 600 miles. An 840-percent increase in growth rate was recorded.[9]

Dr. Miller has developed a standard procedure for measuring the energy from a healer's hands by determining the effect upon the surface tension of water. In honor of the late Ambrose Worrall, who was both a noted healer and scientist, Dr. Miller has named the unit of healer energy the "Worrall" and defines it as the amount of energy required to lower the surface tension of one hundred milliliters of distilled water by ten dynes/centimeter. Ambrose Worrall called this energy "paraelectricity" because, like electricity, it flows from a high-energy source to a person or object at a lower energy level.

As a result of his experiments with Olga Worrall, Dr. Miller has concluded:

1. A primary energy, different from heat, light, or electricity, is emitted from a healer's hands and from magnets.
2. This energy may be detected and quantitatively measured by its effect upon the surface tension of the water.
3. Crystals forming from solutions of cupric chloride will give visual indications of the presence of the energy.
4. Water which has been treated by a healer or a magnet increases the growth rate of plants.
5. Water which has been treated by a healer or a magnet undergoes changes in hydrogen bonding.
6. Energized water is unstable and gives up the excess energy to the environment or to any object in contact with the water.[10]

Dr. Miller's last point concerning energized water may have some implications for the reevaluation of the efficacy of holy water as used in Roman and in some Orthodox churches. If the healing power of Dr. Worrall and others can be transmitted through ordinary water, might not this phenomenon indicate to us what happens when water is sacramentally blessed by the priest?

The late Dr. Schoneberg Setzer, a Research Fellow of the Humanistic Psychology Institute, conducted some interesting experiments with radishes. One sample of radishes was nourished with ordinary water (the control group). The other sample was nourished with water that had been placed in church sanctuaries during worship services. Dr. Setzer found that the effectiveness of the church water varied on a fourteen-day cycle that represented the lunar period. Dr. Edward Brame followed up on Setzer's experiments and had similar results, using infrared spectroscopy to measure quantitative differences between the treated and untreated samples of water. Measurements were taken over a period of weeks both before and after the worship services in various target churches. He also ran a similar test using polimer film with the same results.

1. The water energized in church worship services differed significantly in its molecular activity from the water in the control sample.
2. The degree of the molecular activity varied on a

> fourteen-day lunar cycle with significantly greater
> response at the time of the full and new moon.[11]

(Some will be interested to know that Dr. Brame found no significant difference in the water samples that was indicative of denominational differences!)

From his first finding we see additional evidence for the efficacy of holy water. Furthermore, the results suggest strongly that something physically measurable may take place in a worship experience. Spiritual realities and forces may have concommitant physical manifestations. Dr. Brame's second finding in regard to the lunar cycle's effect upon the treated water indicates that the ancient linking of religious celebrations and rites with phases of the moon may have had a physiological basis, at least in part.

Experiments conducted by Dolores Krieger followed a different approach. Using Colonel Estebany as the healer, she studied the effect of his treatments upon the hemoglobin levels of a test group of patients in comparison with those of an untreated control group. Repeated studies indicated a statistically significant increase in hemoglobin values. A questionnaire follow-up of one group a year later indicated that in most patients the results had prevailed.[12]

A most unusual set of experiments was conducted by Graham and Anita Watkins.[13] Pairs of mice were selected to be rendered unconscious at the same time by use of ether. One of the mice in the pair was to be the subject (comparable to the healee), and the other the untreated control. A volunteer assistant (acting, in a sense, as the healer) was then asked to try to awaken the subject mouse by telepathic means alone (sometimes from within the same room, sometimes at a considerable distance as in absent healing). The volunteer was not allowed to touch the mouse in any way or to make any audible sounds or other sensory stimulation. The findings:

> The overall results of this study were statistically significant; the animals assigned to the volunteers required an average of 13 per cent less time to revive as did the control animals.

There was an additional finding:

Once a mouse revives more quickly than expected by chance, the location of that mouse is recorded. Future mice placed in the same location are more likely to revive quickly than mice placed in other locations—even though the subject does not know about the former inhabitants of that spot. This "lingering effect" suggests that some spots are better than others as locations for "healing," or that a residue of "healing power" remains there to help the next mouse revive.[14]

The implications of this finding for the concept of holy places and sacred ground are obvious.

There is still another kind of research that we need to consider. I have purposely saved it until last, for the process involved in the experiments is the subject of considerable controversy that is not likely to be speedily resolved. The process is called Kirlian photography, named after two Soviet scientists, Semyon and Valentina Kirlian, who greatly helped to pioneer this technique. (It is often erroneously believed that they invented the process, but recent information indicates that the process, using different apparatus, was independently "invented" by various scientists at various times and places.)[15] Kirlian photography is a high-voltage, low-amperage process in which the subject—a fingertip, leaf, or other object—is placed directly upon the photographic plate. The resulting image is a shadowy one of the subject with a corona of colored light, or an aura, surrounding the object, indicating that there is an electrical type of energy that emanates from the subject. This has led some to theorize that there is in addition to the observable physical body an energy body that radiates beyond the limits of the physical body. (This energy body, some have suggested, is what is sometimes represented on religious paintings with the halo and may correspond to Paul's idea of the "spiritual body" in I Corinthians 15.)

Among the first subjects examined by the process of Kirlian photography were leaves. A leaf freshly picked from a tree, it was found, had a larger, more dynamic corona than it would have in the ensuing hours during which it would slowly "die." Some have claimed that the life force—called Spirit or Holy Spirit by Christians; *prana* by Hindus; *mana* by Polynesians; *chi'i* by the

65

Chinese; *ruah* by the ancient Hebrews; astral light by the Kabbalists; *Vis Medicatrix Naturae* by Hippocrates; *pneuma* by Galen; *telesma* by Hermes Trismogistus; *spiritus* by Fludd; magentism by Messmer; mind force by Quimby; and Odic force by Karl von Reichenbach—is manifest in the ebb and flow of the coronas depicted by Kirlian photographs.

Among the earliest Kirlian experiments in the United States with significance for healing were those by Dr. Thelma Moss of U.C.L.A., one of the first American parapsychologists to attempt Kirlian photography after word of its development was brought to the United States by two journalists. Dr. Moss began with a study of the effect of healers upon a leaf as indicated by the Kirlian photographs. Some people, she found, had what she called a "green thumb" effect upon wounded leaves. The energy corona of a wounded leaf was greater after a treatment by a healer than it had been before the healing. She also found that a few people had what she called the "brown thumb" effect; their treatment of a wounded leaf tended to accelerate its decay.

In subsequent experiments with Dr. Worrall and others, she also found that Kirlian photographs of the healer's fingertips before and after a treatment of an object or person indicated that the corona was considerably less after the treatment than before. Together with the evidence that the healee's corona is greater after a treatment, this would seem to indicate that a transfer of energy takes place from the healer to the healee during a treatment.[16]

Some scientists have called into question whether the Kirlian photograph actually depicts an energy corona or simply certain uncontrolled variables, such as body moisture, or poorly controlled variables, such as contact pressure.[17] This controversy will probably continue for some time and until resolved will diminish for the time being the evidential impact of the Kirlian experiments.

Added to the serious case-studies of Kathryn Kuhlman by Allen Spraggett noted at the beginning of this chapter, the research we have been discussing, although it does not prove the validity of spiritual healing, does present some compelling evidence that cannot be ignored or explained away. Science is just beginning to scratch the surface of this vast field of inquiry. Some of the discoveries now being pursued are significantly challenging the world views by which many of us operate, just as the discovery of X rays in 1895, the electron in 1895, radioactivity in 1896, the quantum theory in 1900, and the theory of relativity in 1905 revolutionized all life, not just science. Scientific knowledge is always in a state of flux and change. Some, perhaps much, of what we currently think we know about spiritual healing may also be significantly altered in the years ahead. But spiritual healing in particular, as with religion in general, has nothing to fear from the true scientific mentality that accepts no issue as closed and is perhaps best represented by the reply of Albert Einstein when he was asked how he had discovered the theory of relativity. Without hesitation he said, "I challenged an axiom!"

CHAPTER 8

Alternatives to Healing: Clinging to the Past

The spiritual healer is a thoughtful and realistic prac-
titioner, in no way wishing to displace the medical therapist
but endeavouring, through an appreciation of the spiritual
nature of man, to restore harmony and balance where there
is sickness and pain. In common with all other practition-
ers, it is the aim of the healer to stimulate the natural
processes of healing that, however dormant, lie somewhere
within the patient himself.

—*Gordon Turner,* An Outline of Spiritual Healing

Some years ago I came across a poem that identifies in a vivid
manner one of the greatest obstacles we encounter in a ministry of
healing:

Alternative to Healing

No thing remains alive
That allows its wounds to grow.
If it be plowed, it crops,
Or blows to desert;
If it be body, it heals,
Or starts its sure decay;
If it be all of life together
It finds God,
Or no stitch is strong enough
To be the reconciling.[1]

Most of us tend to think of a wound as something that either
heals or gets worse quite apart from what we want or don't want.
Of course we know that failing to obtain proper medical care may
make our wounds worse, but that is not what the poet is alluding
to. On a much deeper level he is suggesting that often the key to
our health and healing is to be found in our own hands. Although
we frequently assume that the choice between health and sickness

68

is made for us, often we are the ones who choose either wholeness or its alternatives. You and I have far more power over the healing process than we realize, and frequently when our wounds become worse, it is because we have allowed them to do so.

Consider the little boy who falls and cuts his knee. His mother cleans the wound, puts on some antiseptic to kill bacteria, and then covers it with a bandage. Normally, the healing powers of the body will heal that wound in a reasonably short time. If, however, the little boy is constantly tearing off the bandage to see how it is coming along, the healing of the wound will be delayed.

So it is likely to be with many of our ills. Sometimes—in fact, very often—we experience failure in the ministry of healing and the practice of medicine as well because the patient, either consciously or unconsciously, chooses instead of healing, one of its alternatives.

This principle goes far beyond a wounded knee. The obstacle to healing in many areas of life is precisely that we allow our wounds to grow rather than to heal. Illness may prevail, not because disease is inevitable, but because we have chosen an alternative to healing.

My concept of the ministry of healing is not limited to the relief of physical ailments. This ministry must touch all of life, both individual and corporate. People are ill, not only of body, but also of mind and spirit. Our relationships with other people may indicate a brokenness or sickness. Our society and its institutions are often ill. Even the whole world demonstrates a lack of the wholeness for which God created it. The ministry of healing and salvation is intended to bring wholeness wherever we experience brokenness. And often this brokenness of mind, body, spirit, relationships, community, and world comes upon us, not as helpless victims, but as free agents who have knowingly or unknowingly chosen some alternative to healing so that the brokenness is allowed to grow rather than diminish.

For example, we want peace; but, both as individuals and as nations, we make choices that are more likely to move us toward war. We want life, liberty, and justice for all, but we knowingly choose courses that ensure those blessings for a relative few. We want clean air, pure water, and safe communities, but the choices we make are almost certain to poison our air, stagnate our water, and keep our communities in turmoil. Often we are like the politician who, in order to satisfy all his constituents, will vote *for* a particular project but *against* the appropriation bill that would provide its funding.

So it is with us and our health; we want wholeness of mind, body, and spirit, but day after day we may choose the very alternatives to that wholeness, virtually guaranteeing that our wounds will continue to grow.

It has been said, "You can always spot a well-informed man—his views are the same as yours." In the last few years I have been much impressed with the books of Dr. Arnold Hutschnecker, a New York physician whose writings seem to confirm from a medical point of view much of what I have experienced as a pastor and as a participant in the ministry of healing.

In one of his books, *The Will to Happiness,* Dr. Hutschnecker says, "One of the hardest facts for any young doctor to learn is to accept the fact that there are people who don't want to get well—and beyond this, that there are some people who actually want to die." [2]

Ironically, many of these people of whom he is speaking as not wanting to get well are the same people who crowd the physicians' waiting rooms, pastors' studies, and the sanctuaries of healing-ministry churches. One cannot very long be a doctor, pastor, counselor, or healer without realizing that, despite what people may say, do, and even believe, many do not really want to find wholeness.

Unfortunately, many of us learn this the hard way, and some of us seem never to learn it at all.

Ten years ago I began my healing ministry after a period of observing and learning from several fine healers. The very first parishioner upon whom I tried out my new approach to healing was a man in his early seventies. He had been a widower for about two years. Prior to the beginning of his illness he had seemed to be in very good health. Yet, despite the fact that there seemed to be every good reason to expect his recovery, he steadily declined. Determined that he was going to get well, I prayed fervently and believed positively that he would recover.

But he didn't. He died, and that almost finished my ministry of healing before it had actually begun. I could not accept the fact that this apparently robust man could continue to go downhill and die. I so much wanted him to live.

Eventually it dawned upon me that that was the key to my frustration: *I* wanted him to live. But what did *he* want? It should have been obvious to me that he himself had not cared to live. In fact, he had wanted very much to join his departed wife—and did.

Again and again in my ministry I have had to learn that lesson: some people, despite what they may say or do, do not want to get better, for they have consciously or unconsciously chosen an alternative to healing.

What are some of these alternatives?

First of all, some people do not accept healing because they are unwilling to let go of the past. The wound—whether of mind, body, or spirit—does not heal because, like the little boy with the wounded knee, we refuse to keep our hands off the wound.

Often the hurt that is done to us is bad enough. Still, it need not cripple or scar us for life. What scars us, what cripples us, and often what kills us is not the hurt we have received but the hurt we have allowed to grow from that original wound. Left alone or treated normally, the wound would soon heal. Instead, however, it gets worse, much worse, because we allow it to do so. What others do to us is bad enough, but what we do to ourselves with those wounds is often much, much worse.

There is the wound of hostility, for example. I know a man whose life is both literally and figuratively poisoned by his hostility toward his older brother, who as a youth had treated him badly and hurt him very much. Today this man lives only to see retribution come to his brother. He celebrates every misfortune that befalls him. He rejoices in his brother's every mistake and sin. As if it were only yesterday, he can vividly recount every injustice, real or imagined, that his brother caused him. Because he clings to this painful past and lives in a perpetual state of hostility, he has poisoned his own life and cannot find wholeness because he has chosen this alternative that allows the wounds to grow.

The original wounds inflicted upon him obviously are his brother's responsibility; but what he has allowed these wounds to become is his own fault, not his brother's. Strangely, it is not his brother who is suffering from this hostility but himself. Related to this mental and spiritual wound is a serious heart ailment that makes him an invalid. He wants very much to be healed, he says, but he wants to cling to his hostility even more.

Many people are like that man although their circumstances may not be so dramatic. They hold back healing of mind, body, and spirit because they will not let go some wound of the past. They not only remember them, but often they willfully recall them. Once brought to mind, these wounds are held on to, examined, and cherished.

People will not only remember what someone has done to them in the past, but they will relive the incident and savor the emotions of that moment. They will feel again the pain, the anger, the humiliation, the sense of injustice or betrayal. To make certain that they do not forget that wound, they store the memory, ready to call it up at a moment's notice. They catalog other persons' mistakes and remember, word for word, hasty utterances. What someone may say to them in a moment of anger, they immortalize in unforgiving, unforgetting—and unhealing—hearts.

What the mind and heart will not let go, the body in some way records. Anger, jealousy, and bitterness may be recorded in the blood vessels, the heart, the intestines, the muscles, the nervous system, the eyes, the brain, anywhere. And when some part of the body has recorded these deep emotions often enough, sickness or impairment will often result and continue as long as we refuse to let go of the wounds.

Another area in which healing may be thwarted by holding on

to the past is that of guilt. Often it is a deep-seated, sometimes unconscious sense of guilt that is blocking the channel through which healing would be given us.

It is sometimes said—and erroneously, I believe—that Christianity is obsessed with sin and guilt. To the contrary, I believe Christianity strikes the right balance between taking sin either too seriously or not seriously enough. The gospel of Jesus Christ teaches us that the only way to cope with the reality of sin is to deal with it and by the grace of God to put it behind us. Acknowledge it, seek God's forgiveness, and then go on from there in newness of life.

Some people are sick in mind, body, and spirit because they have failed to deal with the reality of sin in a constructive manner. Swept under the carpet, the reality continues to fester and poison life unseen but not unfelt. When we fail to deal with our guilt, we allow the wound to grow.

More than a quarter century ago, the German psychologist Marbe observed that, for many people, having accidents is no accident. It is often a habit, a habitual course of behavior, and the person who has had one accident is more likely to have another accident than the person who has never had one.[3] Often, the key to the habit of accidents is guilt, an unconscious drive to find punishment.

Similarly, Dr. Karl Menninger believes that patients who frequently submit to the surgeon's knife do so as an unconscious expression of guilt. The sufferer, anticipating punishment for his unknown crime, repeatedly offers a part of his body in expiation, hoping that life itself will be spared to him.[4]

With some patients there is an almost aggressive demand for surgery, and this, says Menninger, is a "symptom of the self-destructive force on the rampage."[5] Thus, very often the surgery patient not only lets the wounds grow but insists upon incurring new wounds as well to satisfy the old one that has never been successfully dealt with.

Several years ago on a Sunday morning, a couple drove to my church from a neighboring state. Having read of our healing ministry at Calvary Church, they came hoping I would be able to heal the woman of breast cancer. The woman appeared to be tense and nervous. While she was speaking of her ailment, she chanced to mention her sister. As she spoke the sister's name, a dark, hostile cloud crossed her face. Soon she had forgotten her ailment and spoke at length of her sister's "outrageous actions and attitudes" toward her.

At length I told her that while I could not ascribe her illness to her hostility toward her sister, I nevertheless could say that I did not expect that she would be healed of her cancer so long as this hostility burned so strongly within her. From what she told me it seemed she had every right to be bitter toward her sister. But whether her bitterness was justified, I said, was not the most important thing. Far more important was the fact that her hostility was greatly harming her own well-being. It was a kind of spiritual cancer that continued to eat away at her vitality and to preoccupy her mind.

The woman said she understood and then, without realizing the irony, launched into a ten-minute attack on her sister. Finally, I interrupted her saying, "I don't think you really understood me. If you are going to be freed of this terrible bitterness, then you cannot continue to hold on to it as you are doing right now."

It was obvious that this hostility played a large part in her life, and she was finding it difficult to accept releasing it forever. I suggested that she sit down that very night and write on a tablet all the wrong things her sister had ever done and said to her. "Make sure you get everything down," I instructed her. "Then," I said, "when you have exhausted the subject, I want you to put it in a large ashtray and burn it. As you see that smoke rising out of the flames, tell yourself that you are finished with that subject forever." Reluctantly she agreed.

It is our reluctance to let go the wounds of the past that keeps them alive and growing and prevents us from being whole. We are not healed because we have chosen an alternative to healing.

CHAPTER 9

Alternatives to Healing: Hanging On to the Present

"Really, it has been your thoughts that have made you feel alternatively weak and strong." My guru looked at me affectionately. "You have seen how your health has exactly followed your subconscious expectations. Thought is a force, even as electricity or gravitation. The human mind is a spark of the almighty consciousness of God. I could show you that whatever your powerful mind believes very intensely would instantly come to pass."

—*Paramahansa Yogananda*, Autobiography of a Yogi

One of President Teddy Roosevelt's sons is reported to have said that his father was "all for peace—so long as it didn't interfere with the fighting"!

That is the same way many people think about health: they are all for it so long as it doesn't interfere with something they want even more. Just as some people refuse to allow their wounds to heal by clinging to something in their past, others accomplish the same result by hanging on to the present moment. Their desire for health is secondary to something in their current situation that is actually, although not necessarily admittedly, more important.

There was a woman who regularly came to me for healing of emphysema. She wanted very much to be healed; yet she steadfastly refused to stop smoking as both her physician and I suggested. There was also the alcoholic who desperately wanted to be healed of his affliction—but without giving up the bottle. Or the overweight person who wants to be healed of obesity and hardening of the arteries without going on a diet. Each of these wants healing but also wants something else a great deal more. So the wounds are allowed to grow.

This is the old story of wanting to have your cake and eat it too.

It is a principle observable in many areas of life, not just the ills of the body.

Perhaps your problem is financial—more outgo than income—and you want some healing from your distress but not at the expense of cutting down on your spending or changing your life-style in any way.

Perhaps your brokenness is a ruptured relationship with someone. You wish it were not so, but you are not willing to take the obvious steps required to begin the healing of this relationship.

Perhaps you are greatly concerned about crime in the streets of your community. You deplore this situation and can see that more police and better lighting are necessary. Still, that would require additional funds, meaning more taxes, and you certainly don't want that!

This was the problem with the rich young man who came to Jesus inquiring about eternal life. It seemed this was his greatest goal in life until Jesus advised him to sell his possessions, give the money to the poor, and follow him. As he leaves Jesus with a sad countenance, it is obvious that, although he was interested in seeking eternal life, he wanted his material wealth even more.

Sometimes the choice of the alternative to healing may be very subtle and therefore hidden from our own awareness. We may cling to our brokenness for reasons we will not admit even to ourselves. In his book *The Will to Live,* Arnold Hutschnecker says that "illness is the outer expression of a deep and possibly dangerous struggle going on within." [1] Quite without being aware of it, illness may be a means of coping with a problem that we cannot handle—or at least do not know we can handle—in another, more creative way.

Thus, sickness, accidents, and tragedy may be unconscious choices to escape unpleasant realities. Let us say, for example, that an executive is promoted—along the lines of "the Peter Principle" [2]—to a job that he cannot handle. He is locked into a dilemma: daily it is obvious to him that he is not up to the job, neither can he get out of it. Pride will not allow him to say that it is too much for him. So, he is in one of contemporary society's cul-de-sacs: he can't stay, and he can't go. What's he to do?

At this point, the unconscious comes to his rescue and says, "OK, let's have a heart attack!" He does, and it solves his problem for him. Because of his physical condition, he is excused from the job. In our society we do not look down upon a man who is incapacitated by illness (although we probably would on a man who simply says, "I can't handle it."). The man can always comfort himself with the thought that he could have "done well in that job if it hadn't been for my heart condition." Sickness thus has provided an escape from an unpleasant reality.

Paul Tournier, the distinguished Swiss physician, says that illness may be "a protection against the hurly-burly of life." He has found that often when patients come to him ostensibly to be healed, they proved to be unconsciously afraid of healing. Recovery, he says, "would oblige the sufferer once more to face problems from which his sickness spares him." In *The Meaning of Persons,* Dr. Tournier goes on to catalog his findings:

> A very real and painful migraine, a distressing liver attack, or a stubborn diarrhoea may manifest themselves every time one has to deal with a difficult situation. People who are hard of hearing have confessed to me, too, that they have sometimes been grateful to their infirmity for allowing them to evade an unwelcome dialogue.[3]

Sickness and impairment may also be unconscious means of securing love and attention that we believe we cannot obtain in any other manner. In his autobiographical book, *Surprised by Joy,* C. S. Lewis tells of being spared service in the trenches of World War I by a sickness called trench fever. "Perhaps I ought to have mentioned before," he writes, "that I had had a weak chest ever since childhood and had very early learned to make a minor illness one of the pleasures of life."[4]

Lots of people have made that same discovery. What child has not at some time given the impression of being considerably more ill than was actually the case because of the love and special attention malaise seemed to bring? In that respect, some people never grow up; they have become so accustomed to getting love and attention in that manner that they are unwilling to risk getting it in any other way.

Dr. Hutschnecker gives us an interesting case study in *The Will to Live:*

> An elderly man, a grandfather, came to me with peptic ulcers from which he had been suffering for thirty years, the major part of his adult life. If he could only be rid of them! It was all he asked of life, he said.
>
> "Suppose tomorrow you woke up cured—what would you do?" I asked him.
>
> "Why, I would enjoy life," he answered.
>
> "How would you enjoy it? What would you do?" I persisted.
>
> 'Why—" he floundered, "I would enjoy it—like other people."
>
> He could not be more specific. He had no plan, no purpose, no driving desire to be well in order to accomplish something that was important to him. For thirty years he had built his life around this illness. His colleagues in business catered to him, praised him for his devotion to his work despite his handicap. His family at home cushioned him with attentions because of his "condition." The bowl of hot soup was always waiting for him when he got home from the office.
>
> To take away his ulcer would at one sweep deprive him of the special position he enjoyed, and all the attentions which served him in place of mature relationships of mutual affection and responsibility. Take away his ulcer and you take away the bowl of hot soup, *his substitute for love*. No, he could not say he would enjoy life without his ulcer. He needed his ulcer. [italics mine][5]

Hutschnecker's analysis of the case study above has been confirmed many times in my work as both pastor and healer. People are often unconsciously unwilling to give up their illness because in a perverted way they need their sickness. They have given up the opportunity for mature loving relationships for the sake of commanding love and attention in a way learned in their childhood.

A man once came to me after he had divorced his alcoholic wife. They had come to the point where the life of the whole family was revolving around the wife's alcoholism. They tiptoed through their daily lives trying desperately not to upset the precarious balance of periodic sobriety and ensuing pleasantness. Finally, when it seemed he could stand it no longer, he decided that divorce was the lesser of two evils.

Yet, having at last found his release from that dissipating relationship, what was he doing in my study? As he talked, it soon became clear that he now missed greatly that "life of misery" that had seemed so unbearable. The major purpose—playing the martyr to an alcoholic spouse—had gone out of his life. He no longer felt needed, because no one was entirely dependent upon him anymore. Thus, he confessed, he had begun to see his ex-wife again because, without realizing it as such, he needed her illness.

Sickness may also be a means of exercising power over others. Often there is no worse tyrant than the impatient patient, for our illness may be the means we employ to make other people do what we want them to do. I once knew a woman who always had a heart attack whenever her son became serious with a girl and talked of marriage. I do not mean that these heart attacks were faked—they were certainly real enough from a medical point of view—but they were nevertheless an unconscious attempt to maintain control over the son. And the method was quite successful a number of times until one day the son decided to get married despite the risk. Once again his mother had a heart attack, but she survived, long enough to die a considerable number of years later of something quite unrelated.

Fear may also lie at the heart of a person's illness. Strange as it may seem, some people become so accustomed to their illness that they unconsciously cling to the misery they know rather than take their chances with an unknown hope. Their illness has become their security blanket, insulating them from the risks of mature living. This may constitute a physical illness, a bad case of nerves, a broken relationship in the home, a tragic circumstance, or a neurotic pattern of behavior. At least it is familiar, and because it is familiar, no matter how painful, they have learned to live with it.

I knew a couple who had a severely brain-damaged daughter.

They refused to even consider placing the child in a special-care facility, even when it became apparent that that would probably be best for everyone concerned, particularly a younger, normal child. When questioned about their attitude, the wife confessed that the daughter's impairment was the only thing holding the marriage together.

How tragic that so many people become accustomed to sickness and misery, continuing to hold on to it long after the original necessity has been served. If you've read Charles Dickens' *A Tale of Two Cities,* you may remember the cobbler who spent a long time in the darkness of a French dungeon. Freed at last, he went to England and built himself a home. Strangely, however, he made the heart of his new home very much like the dark cell that he had left behind in France. Secluded there from the outside world which frightened him, he spent his days shielded from the bright sunlight, and one could hear from the darkness of his cell-like home that tap-tap of his cobbler's hammer. He had been released from jail, but he was still a prisoner of his fear. As he had become fearful of freedom, so many of us may be fearful of wholeness and thus choose an alternative to it.

Illness may serve still another purpose: the maintenance of what we might call the "Hercules syndrome." These are people who take a perverted pride in what they regard as weaknesses of Herculean proportions. The apostle Paul said, "When I am weak, then I am strong" (II Cor. 12:10), but he meant that in the recognition of his weakness he found the sufficiency of God's power. Instead, many people find their weakness as the source of a perverted strength; they see their weakness, their faults, their sins, their illnesses as so gigantic that they conquer the positive strength of the strong, including God himself. Unable to compete in a positive manner, these people take satisfaction in being so sick, so helpless, so hopeless, that they utterly overwhelm and defeat anyone who would try to heal or help them.

This is truly a blasphemous state of mind, for it says to God, "Lord I'm a bigger sinner than you are a forgiver; my weakness is greater than your power; my sickness is stronger than your power to heal; my problem is too big for you to solve; and the mess I'm in is too much for even you to straighten out." Without realizing it, the person is saying, "I have contended with Almighty God himself, and I, in my weakness, have prevailed!"

In the ministry of healing we must realize that we cannot help that kind of person until or unless he or she wants to be helped. These people will simply play games with us and will find their secret delight in sending us away frustrated and defeated in our attempts to help them. Playing that game is good neither for them nor us.

A few years ago I visited the city of Jerusalem and viewed the ruins of what is identified as the Pool of Bethesda. As I stood there, I could not help remembering the incident in chapter 5 of the Gospel According to John of Jesus' healing a crippled man. I used to regard that as a pretty incredible story, for John tells us that the man had been impaired for thirty-eight years and had lain by that pool waiting for a healing. It was believed that periodically an angel would come and trouble the waters of the pool, and if someone could lower himself into the pool at that time, he would be healed.

Unfortunately, said the man, every time the pool was troubled by the angel, people rushed in front of him, and, without help, he never made it there in time. Thirty-eight years, and he had never gotten to the pool in time! That seemed incredible to me.

Yet, as I stood there, it dawned upon me that Jesus found it just as incredible as I did, and this is why he asked what must have seemed a strange question: "Do you want to be healed?"

Did he want to be healed? Is Jesus cruelly jesting with him? Why would he have lain there so long if he hadn't wanted to be healed? But Jesus knew what he was asking the man. Here at last was an opportunity for the man to be healed, to stop living on excuses, blaming others, and playing the role of the poor martyr. Was he ready to give up that role and assume a responsible place in the community?

There is no more important question for the healer to ask, and we must be cautious of glib answers too easily given, for often they are unconsciously fraudulent. A physician I know was approached by a patient who said he'd do anything he had to do if he could be freed of a certain malady. He'd take any medication, submit to any surgery; and price was no object. After a thorough examination and battery of laboratory tests, the physician prescribed a rigorous program that had been very successful with other patients suffering the same malady. When confronted with this program, however, the patient who said he'd "do anything" to be well, answered with a promise to "think about it." He never returned. He wanted healing but not that much.

There is an old story about a religious man who walked throughout India seeking "the key to salvation." One day after many fruitless months and miles he came to a holy man who, upon hearing his customary question, took him down to the Ganges River. Wading out into the midst of the river to waist depth, the holy man suddenly thrust the seeker's head into the water and held it there. Struggling desperately, the seeker felt his lungs about to burst when the holy man pulled him quickly to the surface. As the seeker gulped in the precious air, the holy man asked him, "While I held your head under the water, what did you want?" "Air!" gasped the seeker, "more than I've ever wanted anything else!" "Yes," responded the holy man, "and when you want salvation as much as you wanted air, you will find it."

So, it seems to me, Jesus says both to us and to those to whom we would minister, "Do you want to be healed?" If you do, if you really do, then you can no longer hold on to your wounds, your power over others, your fears, your excuses, your cop-outs, your familiar miseries, but you must take the risk of finding wholeness and the fullness of life that will elude you unless you desire them deeply enough.

CHAPTER 10

Why Isn't Everyone Healed? and Other Hard Questions

Only a physician who believes in a potential power for healing that exists within his patient can treat his patient. Whether he calls this power the vis medicatrix naturae *(healing power of nature) or the* vis medicatrix dei *(healing power of God), the worthy physician has faith that the patient is fighting alongside him for health and against sickness. In a sense the physician can be only the assistant to this power, saying with Ambrose Paré, the "Father of French Surgery," "I dressed his wounds and God healed him," or with Sigmund Freud, the father of psychoanalysis, that we are midwives participating in the birth of the healthy self.*

—*Earl A. Loomis, Jr.,* The Self in Pilgrimage

In my years of healing ministry, there have been dramatic successes and inspiring demonstrations of the healing love and power of God in Jesus Christ. In a book such as this there is a natural tendency to speak about these rather than the failures. Nevertheless, we must face up to the hard questions that apparent failure to heal raises in the minds of ourselves and others.

When we do so, it seems to me that we cannot help but confess that, despite all that we do know about spiritual healing, we must also confess that much of this subject is still a great mystery. There is much that we do not understand about healing, and anyone who says he or she has all the answers is simply not being honest.

This is nowhere more true than with the question of why everyone is not healed. What follows is a list of possible, although not exhaustive, answers that may be offered in response to it.

Actually, we have already indicated at least one answer in chapters 8 and 9. People sometimes choose, consciously or unconsciously, to hold on to their illness. This may or may not be apparent to others. Thus, we may be baffled because a patient fails to respond to our therapy, little realizing that the patient wants something else more than healing and wholeness.

We have also suggested previously that people continue to surround themselves with the same influences that led them into illness. You cannot maintain certain practices and hope to be successful in seeking healing, medical or spiritual. To continue smoking when there is good reason to believe that smoking was one of the primary agents in making you ill, is foolish. Yet, many people do just that.

Another answer to this big question may be found in our tendency to deal with symptoms rather than causes. Although healing is often most helpful in relieving symptoms, that is hardly where we need to focus. If there is discord in the home that results in a severe case of arthritis, it will do little good to treat the arthritic pains and leave the domestic strife unresolved.

We must also remember that spiritual healing is not magic. As we have already indicated, it works through natural laws of which at the present we know very little. But there is no waving of a magic wand to suspend the operation of the universe so that our own purposes may be served. If the root cause of our illness has been a deep sense of guilt, we can not guarantee that, once discovered and dealt with, the symptoms will automatically disappear. Although an overpowering sense of guilt may impede the effective operation of our immunizing system and therefore make us susceptible to a particular virus, once given a foothold, the disease may continue well after we have dealt with the spiritual problem, particulary if the disease has seriously weakened the body, damaged various organs, cells, and tissues. Harry Edwards, a reknowned British healer, puts it this way:

> If the help of spiritual healing is asked for in a case of advanced cancer, it may be that the physical resistance of the patient has become so weak, that *in the time available* it is not possible to re-stimulate the resources of the body sufficiently to fight the effects. [italics mine][1]

Another reason that healing may be blocked or retarded is that the patient is surrounded by an atmosphere that is unreceptive and hostile to healing. As spiritual healing is not magic, neither is the healer a magician, but rather a channel through which God is able to dispense his healing power. The amount of power that is directed through that healing channel must be mounted in opposition to the power of the disease. But if there are people around the patient who are quite unreceptive to the possibility of the patient's cure, the effectiveness of the healer may be greatly diminished. Through their negativity, people may greatly augment the destructive power of illness.

I have frequently been asked to pray for patients whose death had already been accepted as likely by friends and family members. These patients are most difficult to help, for, although I may be successful in putting them in a receptive, hopeful frame of mind, my visits have been literally undone by others who unconsciously inflict the patient with their own skepticism. I have found that there are incidents in the New Testament where Jesus asked to be alone with the patient. Very likely he believed that he would be more effective as a healer if certain people were absent!

It has often shocked me to hear the change that takes place in the way people speak of someone once they have learned that the person has been stricken with a serious disease, like cancer. Without realizing it, they begin to speak of that person who is still alive in the past tense: "Poor John, he *was* such a great guy." God protect John from these friends who unwittingly have already written him off.

Sometimes we are ineffectual in healing because we do not give God enough of ourselves with which to work. A disease of great magnitude may require more than just a three-minute prayer and laying on of hands. In healing, as in many of God's activities in this world he has created, God works through people who serve as his channels. If we do not give him enough of our time and attention, he may be limited in what can be accomplished through us. Sometimes, I believe, our prayers are too fleeting and vague to be of much help with conditions that require concentrated power.

There are also other times when healing prayer may be

ineffective because we are too specific and narrow in our receptivity. We may not only want God to heal the condition, but we may become so intent that the healing take place in but one specific way, that we block the channel through which God would give us the healing power. This is when we refuse to let God be God and determine how he will achieve his will in and through us.

Another reason for seeming ineffectiveness in healing is our failure to grasp that the healing of the physical body is not the highest of all goals. Dr. Elizabeth Milne, a British physician, has said that ''we so often tend to think of illness as the worst thing that can befall us . . . whereas most of us here would realize that there are things far harder to bear and far more crippling than pain and sickness.'' [2] Most spiritual healers, perhaps all, agree that the most important object sought in healing is the healing of the spirit. Often there can be physical healing only when the spirit has been healed.

It is often true, too, that a patient will be healed in spirit although for one or more reasons cited above the body will not be healed. Emily Gardner Neal helps us to see this in perspective:

> No one who properly understands spiritual healing ever turns from God because he is not healed, for no one who turns to Him in faith remains unhealed spiritually. Further, no one who has experienced a healing of the spirit would exchange what he has received for a purely physical cure. [3]

In the next chapter we will examine yet another reason we may experience seeming failure in spiritual healing.

Why Are the Wrong People Healed Sometimes?

Sometimes people whom we would judge worthy of healing are not helped physically, while others who seem unlikely subjects for God's help are healed. This is hardly a new opinion, for Jesus himself was probably accused of healing the ''wrong'' people, just as he was criticized for association with the ''wrong'' people. Actually, there seems to be a validity in this claim, for a considerable number of Jesus' healings are given to people whom we would judge to be unlikely recipients: obvious sinners; people who have not been very religious, who have come from other religious backgrounds; foreigners; people who have little or no doctrinal knowledge of Jesus and his identity as the Messiah, the Son of God. Jesus refused to perform his ministry of healing and salvation according to the expectations and presuppositions of both his friends and enemies.

So it is that God may deal with us in our ministry of healing and help. He may refuse to play by our rules, accept our judgments as to who is worthy or unworthy of his power, or restrict himself to man-made parameters. Despite how much we know or think we know, God may insist upon being God and working in ways that are both mysterious and disturbing to us.

When Allen Spraggett interviewed the late Kathryn Kuhlman, one of the best-known healers in the United States, she told him:

I have decided that God doesn't have preferences in theology. . . . We are the ones who try to put a fence around God, to bring him down to our level. But it doesn't work. God is too big for us to confine. . . . There was a day, when I was very young and knew a great deal more than I do now, that I said, "You must do thus and so, to be healed. There are certain conditions that have to be met." I thought, for example, that faith on the part of the seeker was absolutely necessary.

Then one day I got the shock of my life. A man said his deaf ear had just been opened in a service, but he had no faith at all. "I don't believe in it," he said. "I never go to church." *Well, there went my theology out the window.* [italics mine][4]

God has an absolute talent for kicking my theology out the window, particularly when I am confident that I have pretty well figured him out.

Thus, we cannot explain why sometimes God seems to heal the "wrong" people, but perhaps one answer or a portion of it may lie in the difference between the conscious and unconscious minds. We are not always what we seem to be, even to ourselves! We may be like the two sons in the parable that Jesus told: upon being told to work in the vineyard, the one son said, "I will not," but did so later, while the other said, "I will," but never did. One man may say, "I believe," but unconsciously he may be so fearful that he cannot receive the gift of healing. Another may say, "I don't believe in all that garbage," but deep, down inside he may be more receptive than the first man. He may be so accustomed to playing a role—the self-sufficient man, the village agnostic, the scientific man who needs no "superstition," etc.—that he is not in contact with his own inner realities.

Thus, some of the answer as to why God seems to heal the "wrong" people is probably to be found in the mysteries of the unconscious mind. In exploring that dimension in his book *Christian Life and the Unconscious,* Dr. Ernest White, a physician who worked closely with Dr. Leslie Weatherhead at City Temple in London, told of a British clergyman and a sailor who lay in adjacent beds in a hospital ward. Both delirious, the clergyman was heard to curse, while the sailor continued to pray![5]

I was once asked to see a woman who had lost a son to a disease that struck him down without warning in his early years of young adulthood. It soon became apparent, however, that my counseling was to no avail, and despite her desire for help, the woman was not able to rise above her doubts. Finally, I indicated this to her and said that I was sorry but that I didn't feel that I was likely to be of help to her. She amicably agreed and stopped coming to me.

Some months later, a friend of hers called me and told me that the woman, whom we'll call Mrs. Thomas, was in the hospital for surgery to remove a growth on her neck. Would I please visit her, her friend requested. Remembering how ineffective I had been with Mrs. Thomas, I reluctantly agreed.

Greeting her as I entered the hospital room, I said, "Your friend suggested you might want me to pray for you." "Sure," Mrs. Thomas replied good-naturedly (her skepticism was never hostile), "why not? It can't do any harm." With that encouragement, I placed my hands on the growth, prayed briefly and beat a hasty retreat. I had done what I was asked to do, but I didn't expect anything would happen. Mrs. Thomas was too doubtful, I was sure.

The next day her friend called me and informed me that the operation had been postponed. It seemed that when the doctor visited Mrs. Thomas later that same day when I had called on her, he found that the growth on her neck had shrunk some, and he decided to postpone surgery until it was determined what would happen. I was incredulous at this news but even more so a day or two later when the same friend informed me that Mrs. Thomas had been discharged from the hospital. The reason: the growth had disappeared! Of all people I thought might be likely recipients, Mrs. Thomas, the pleasant skeptic, seemed one of the most unlikely. Apparently, God knew something that I didn't!

Is Spiritual Healing the Same as Faith Healing?

My answer is a definite no, although I have to acknowledge that this question can get bogged-down in semantics. Many of us in this ministry avoid the term *faith healing* because of the unfortunate connotations it may convey to people. For some people it may suggest the kind of emotionally excessive tent meeting that so turned me off as a seminary student. Those of us who want to bring the ministry of healing back into the churches do not want to identify with the commercialized, exploitive, faith healing image.

Even more important, however, is the fact that the term *faith healing* indicates that healing is a reward given in exchange for the right amount of faith. As we have already indicated, sometimes healing may take place when the patient seems quite lacking in faith. Furthermore, although it is desirable that the patient be receptive, healing, like salvation, is a matter of grace. We do not earn our healing with our doctrines and creeds. No one is *worthy* to be healed. It is God's gift.

The term *faith healing* also suggests that if a person is not healed, the reason is a deficiency of faith, whereas we have already indicated that there may be many reasons for our failure to be healed.

Isn't It Selfish to Ask God to Heal You?

If it were just your desire to be well, that might be true. But remember, God wants you to be whole; in fact, he wants it even

89

more than you do. Therefore, to seek wholeness is not selfish but is a desire that is perfectly in accordance with God's own will. What may be selfish is our demand that God heal us in the way we desire and according to our own timetable.

How Do We Know that Some Healing Is Not the Work of the Devil?

Some people of particular religious persuasions make it a practice to cast doubt on the authenticity of some healing ministries, particularly when those ministries represent a religious style other than their own. I have been told by well-meaning people; "When we heal, it is the work of the Holy Spirit; but when you heal, how can we be sure you are not being used by Satan?"

Well-meaning or not, these people are dangerous to others and to themselves. They fail to realize that virtually the same charge was hurled at Jesus by his pharasaical opponents: "It is only by Beelzebul, the prince of demons, that this man casts out demons." Jesus ridiculed this charge, reminding them that "every kingdom divided against itself is laid waste." In other words, it is ridiculous to assume that Satan would work with Jesus in destroying Satan's own work—illness and possession. But Jesus goes on to make a somber charge that ought to sober all of us who are inclined to cast doubt on the ministry of others: "Every sin and blasphemy will be forgiven men, but the blasphemy against the Spirit will not be forgiven" (see Matt. 12:22–32). A person will endanger his own soul when he takes it upon himself to suggest that God's work through someone else is actually the work of the devil! And that is precisely what we are in danger of doing when we point the finger at those whom we do not understand or with whom we do not agree.

Even the Sanhedrin was made to realize this. As Peter and John stood before this ruling body in Jerusalem, one of the rabbis, Gamaliel, prevailed upon the Sanhedrin with these words: "Men of Israel, take care what you do with these men. . . . If this plan or this undertaking is of men, it will fail; but if it is of God, you will not be able to overthrow them. *You might even be found opposing God!*" (Acts 5:35–39; emphasis added).

Jesus told his disciples that the validity of their ministry would be determined by their "fruits." "A sound tree cannot bear evil fruit, nor can a bad tree bear good fruit," said Jesus (Matt. 7:18–20). And at another time when the disciples of John came to him, saying, "Teacher, we saw a man casting out demons in your name, and we forbade him, because he was not following us," Jesus pointedly replies, "Do not forbid him; for no one who does a mighty work in my name will be able soon after to speak evil of me. For he that is not against us is for us" (Mark 9:38–40).

We hear much today about "counterfeit miracles" and suspicions about the devil lurking behind every pulpit, but we do not find these concerns coming from the words of Jesus in the Four Gospels. Jesus tells us to focus upon people's fruits rather than their words. Unfortunately, there are those today who seem obsessed with the devil. They see him everywhere (except in their own church or group, of course!). In fact, they seem to know more of and speak more about Satan than they do God. Their constant anxiety about the demonic in other people seems to imply a lack of faith in God. If they are that afraid of Satan, they can hardly trust fully in God. Oddly enough, it is these people who spend so much time wondering about everyone else who seem to be Satan's best press agents. They keep his name before the public and give him the kind of publicity that God alone should have.

Aren't There Dangers in Spiritual Healing?

Of course there are, just as there are dangers in practically any Christian endeavor. In writing to the church at Corinth, Paul indicates that the wrong attitude in taking Holy Communion can actually produce both sickness and death. But he does not counsel the Corinthians to give up the Lord's Supper, only their wrong attitude (see I Cor. 11:1–32).

Jesus warns of the danger of praying and fasting with a showy and proud spirit, but he does not suggest that his disciples give up either of these spiritual disciplines (see Matt. 6:1–18).

91

In spiritual healing there is always the danger that people will become fixed upon sheer physical satisfaction, that having received their healing they will not give God the thanks and praise, that the healer will become proud and vain because of what God has accomplished through him. But none of these dangers need be fatal to the ministry of spiritual healing.

What Is the Relation of the Healing Ministry to the Charismatic Movement?

Much depends upon what you mean by *charismatic movement*. Unfortunately the public has associated the word *charismatic* (meaning a gift from God) with a particular movement, called by some the "Neo-Pentacostals" and known particularly for glossalalia or, speaking in tongues. I believe that genuine gifts of the Spirit are to be found in this movement, including spiritual healing, but we need to realize that the gifts of the Spirit are available to all Christians, not just those who are in this movement. Speaking in tongues may surely be a valid gift of the Holy Spirit, but the New Testament places a much higher value on healing than upon tongue-speaking. The apostle Paul seems to place this charisma near the bottom of his list (see I Cor. 12:4–11) and, although he acknowledges that he has spoken in tongues himself, says, "Nevertheless, in church I would rather speak five words with my mind, in order to instruct others, than ten thousand words in a tongue" (I Cor. 14:19).

The movement for the ministry of spiritual healing may include but also goes far beyond the so-called Neo-Pentacostalist movement.

How Does Death Fit In with the Ministry of Spiritual Healing?

Let's move on to the next chapter and consider that important question.

CHAPTER 11

Learning to Die

It is like the story told of Forain, the French painter, who became ill and was examined by half a dozen specialists. The heart specialist pronounced his heart in good shape, the lung specialist declared his lungs to be fine, the kidney specialist reported that his kidneys were functioning properly, and so on until Forain broke in: "Then, gentlemen, it seems that I am dying in perfect health!"

—Arnold Hutschnecker, The Will to Live

Several years ago there appeared on network television a two-part documentary on the life and work of Leonardo da Vinci. Late in his life, he was quoted as saying, "All these years I thought I was learning to live, but instead I've been learning to die!"

For most persons the idea of learning to die may seem strange, for it appears to be something we just do. But death is not so simple; it is complex and deeply significant. Thus, several years before his own death, Dag Hammarskjöld, then secretary general of the United Nations, wrote these words:

> The hardest thing of all—to die rightly—
> An exam nobody is spared—and how many pass it?[1]

Christianity is not only a way of life but also a way of death, and learning "to die rightly" has always been one of the aims of Christian discipleship, regardless of how successful we may feel we have been in that endeavor.

So where does the experience of death fit in with the ministry of healing? It would seem that death would be an embarassing reminder that this ministry is often not effective. Instead, however, it is a reminder that no participant in this ministry must ever forget: all physical healings, medical or spiritual or both, are only temporary!

93

In other words, we are all going to die of something someday. The body is not designed to live forever. We will be taking it off someday like a suit of old clothes that is baggy and threadbare. But this is not a tragedy, as we may think, for the apostle Paul indicates that having shed the physical body, we will put on another, this time an everlasting form.

In the minds of many people, death is regarded as the ultimate tragedy. Yet in light of our Christian beliefs and expectations, death ought to be regarded as *the ultimate healing*. It is not a tragic and ignoble end to life, a "rotten break that overtakes us," but a blessed part of God's plan and purpose for this world. Death represents not the thwarting of his game plan but really the fulfillment of it.

Often it is only through this ultimate healing of death that a person can finally know the wholeness for which he or she was created. A person who has had to struggle through life with the burden of amputation, loss of vision, or some other vital faculty, will be fully healed only through that transition we call death.

So, sometimes in our ministry of healing we must help people to learn to die "rightly," as Hammarskjöld put it. But it is not easy, for our society has great difficulty in dealing with the meaning of death. In fact, thanatologist Elizabeth Kübler-Ross says that ours is a death-denying society. For many, she says, "death is viewed as a taboo, discussion of it is regarded as morbid, and children are excluded with the presumption and pretext that it would be 'too much' for them." [2]

Many pastors have faced this frustrating situation: the patient knows he is dying, but the family pledges a conspiracy to "keep Dad from knowing we know." The pastor is forbidden to even mention death to the patient and is thus robbed of an opportunity to help the patient in preparing for one of his most important experiences. The strain on the patient is great: courageously he strives to help the family keep the illusion of maintaining absolute silence. Small wonder that many regard death as man's ultimate tragedy, that they die as victims instead of the victors they were created to be.

So, for many, the experience is a far cry from the victory painted on the pages of the New Testament. L. P. Jacks has written:

> No religion is worth its name unless it can prove itself more than a match for death. . . . Christianity came into the world as a death-conquering religion. It centered on the figure of a death-conqueror.[3]

Actually, strange as it may seem, one of the greatest privileges in the ministry of healing is that of helping someone to die! One of my first experiences of this type took place in Bronxville, a suburb of New York City. As a local minister, it was my duty to visit the hospital every other week as chaplain for the day. This involved calling on patients who had not specified a religious affiliation. It usually consisted of a brief visit, an offer to contact a clergyman of the faith of their preference, and a prayer. Sometimes, of course, the visits were more extended than that.

On this particular day I was given the card of an old gentleman with a Germanic name. Upon entering the room I saw a bed surrounded by an anxious and weary family. The elderly man in the bed was in a coma, and they said he had been that way for several days. It was time to die, the doctor had told them, and they believed their grandfather wanted to die but for some reason couldn't seem to let go.

Sensing that I was wondering about praying for him, one of them said, "Why don't you pray for him? Even though he can't hear you, maybe somehow he'll know you're doing it." Inquiring about his religious background, I found that he had not been in the United States long but had come here from his native Berlin just a few years ago. "Does he speak English?" I asked. "Yes," they replied, "but, of course, if only you could pray for him in German—if anything would get through to him, that would!"

Although I had had some high-school German and had grown up in the Pennsylvania Dutch culture (German, actually), I knew I couldn't pray in German. But as I began to apologize, I suddenly remembered that I had once learned the Lord's Prayer in German from an old German Bible. So, haltingly I prayed: *"Unser Vater, in dem Himmel . . ."*

When I was finished, the family joined in to thank me. One of them said, "Grandad seemed to stir a little as you prayed; I think he heard you." I wasn't able to discern any response, but I was satisfied that they seemed happy with what little I had been able to do. Leaving them my card, I left the hospital and returned to my study. I had been barely seated a few minutes when the phone rang. It was one of the members of the German man's family. "We thought you'd want to know," he said, "You were gone only about fifteen minutes when Grandad passed over." Then, as I was digesting this, he added; "We are so grateful for what you did for him: we're sure that your prayer helped him to die."

His words sent a chill through me—helped him to die! Is that what I had done? How awful to think that I had contributed in some way to the loss of that old man! It seemed a terrible verdict upon my hospital ministry.

Yet, as I turned those words over in my mind, I began to view the whole experience differently. The doctor had said it would be tragic for him to continue to hang on by a thread, which he had been doing to the impoverishment of his family. They had felt that he was ready to die and wanted to make the transition. Instead of viewing my ministry as a failure, therefore, I began to see it in a different light, and I was glad that God had let me share in this high moment.

Today I have no hesitation in helping a patient to die. That doesn't mean that I am involved in any way in that decision. In fact, I have found that we do not have to become involved. But knowing that it is a possibility, at times even a probability, we can play a part in making it a victorious experience.

A number of years ago I was called late on a Saturday night by a parishioner. The teen-aged son of a friend of hers had been in a terrible auto accident. The car had rolled over, and the boy had been thrown out on the road surface. Most of the impact had been absorbed by his head. The result was a fractured skull, concussion, and internal injuries. He had lain in intensive care for five days, never opening his eyes, moving, or making a sound. Worst of all, he had sustained extensive brain damage; even if he did recover, which seemed unlikely the doctors said, he could hardly be anything more than "a vegetable." "Would you be able to go to see him tonight? I know it's late, but it would mean so much to the family."

I drove to the hospital and beat a familiar path to the Intensive Care Unit. I had never met the boy, but even if I had, I suppose I wouldn't have been able to recognize him. There was nowhere to place my hands, so I held them above him as I prayed and committed him to God's care.

Leaving the room, I met his stricken family in the waiting room. I comforted them as best I could and decided that I would ask my congregation the next morning during the Sunday service to take some special moments to pray for him.

Just before I was scheduled to preach the morning sermon, I stepped into the pulpit and shared my concern for the boy and his family with the congregation. Some of the people present knew the family, but most did not. Still, there was a wave of compassion and concern rising from the pews. I told them we were going to pray for the boy, but I said that first I wanted to help them to understand how we ought to pray for him. I briefly explained his condition and outlined the possible alternatives.

"Now," I said, "you may wonder just how you ought to pray for him. Should we pray for God to help him to live, even though we know how tragic his continuing life is likely to be? Or, should we ask God to take his life so that neither he nor his family will have to risk such a tragic existence?" The answer, I said, was neither of these. "God wants him whole even more than you and I do," I said, "but at this point God alone knows wherein that wholeness lies: whether in continued life here on earth or in a life beyond death. Let us commit him to God's hands and ask that his healing will may be done." We continued for a few moments in silence until I pronounced the amen.

Following the service, a considerable number of parishioners told me that they had never known how to pray for someone who is close to death. This matter had always bothered them, and they were glad that I had helped them to see that they could pray for healing without attempting to play God. (Ironically, the boy's family called me later that day and told me their son had passed away quietly late that morning, approximately five minutes after we had prayed for his healing. I would not claim a causal correspondence between the two events, but neither would I want to deny the possibility.)

I have always been convinced that much of the effectiveness of our weekly healing service was dependent upon the teaching seminar that just preceded it every Thursday morning. In this informal setting I tried to prepare people's attitudes and expectations: the better prepared they were, I found, the more likely they were to find the healing helpful to them.

Included in this preparation was always some attempt to present the experience of death as the ultimate healing. Actually, I found that when people faced the reality of death, they were often much more receptive to healing. Fear and anxiety can very much interfere with recovery from illness. When people deal with death in a realisitc manner, they are enabled to divert their energies to recovery instead of fighting a running battle with fears.

The fear of death is definite detriment to healing, medical or spiritual. There is an old Arab legend about a caravan that met Pestilence upon the way to Baghdad. "Why," asked the Arab chieftain, "must you hasten to Baghdad?" Pestilence replied, "To take five thousand lives!" Later, upon returning from Baghdad, the caravan once again encountered Pestilence in the desert. "You deceived me," the chieftain said angrily. "Instead of five thousand lives, you took fifty thousand!" "Nay," replied Pestilence, "five thousand and not one more. It was Fear who killed the rest!"

So, the writer of the Epistle to the Hebrews tells us, "He himself likewise partook of the same nature, that through death he might destroy him who has the power of death, that is, the devil, and *deliver all those who through fear of death were subject to lifelong bondage*" (Heb. 2:14–15; italics mine).

The ministry of healing must help people so that they may be delivered of this lifelong bondage: the fear of death. It is often this fear which makes it both hard to live and hard to die.

I have always enjoyed receiving letters that speak of dramatic recoveries. But one of the most satisfying letters I have ever received was in another vein entirely. It was from a Long Island pastor who just two weeks previously had visited our healing service with a parishioner whose wife, the physicians had said, was dying.

I had taken them into my study following the service because I wanted to get a better idea of why they had made such a long drive. They explained the situation: the wife was dying of cancer, and there seemed to be no hope. They had read of a "miraculous healing" of a woman who had cancer, and they had hoped against hope that we might do the same with this good wife. We talked for a long time about healing, including about death as the ultimate healing, before they had to begin their long journey home. I hoped they wouldn't feel their trip had been in vain.

Several weeks later, I received this letter from the pastor:
Dear Mr. Althouse:

I write to express thanks for the help we received with you and from you at the seminar and service on November 14th—and for your kindness in taking the time to visit with Heinz Fetche, and his son, Karl, and me in your office after the informal group conversation in the chapel. The day in Mohnton was a time of quiet healing for us, and remembering the part of our conversation that considered death as a kind of final healing, it was also for Anna Fetche, the wife of Heinz.

Anna Fetche died at home early in the morning of November 21st, just one week after our visit in Mohnton. It was a quiet passing. She never had, so far as I knew, any hard pain; and was not under any unusual sedation at any time. The two daughters . . . were with Heinz in the room at the bed at the last. Anna looked at them from her bed, so they told me, smiled a "beautiful smile" and then, half an

99

hour later, was gone with no further "communication." Perhaps there was a kind of communication the next night. Heinz has told me that he and his son . . . were alone in the bedroom the next night, when for no apparent reason there was a strong and pronounced vibration of a picture over the head of the bed—so much so that he placed his hand against the picture frame. He thought perhaps it was a kind of "word" from Anna.

Again for your ministry at the church, and that of the others who were there, and for your personal concern—we are grateful.

We can help death to be both a healing experience and a victory if we will help people to change their attitudes toward this experience. It is at death that often the patient can be closest to the Healing Christ. Everything depends upon our own attitudes and expectations.

Teilhard de Chardin, the Roman Catholic priest and scientist, once prayed, "Grant me, then, something even more precious than that grace for which all your faithful followers pray: to receive communion as I die is not sufficient: *teach me to make a communion of death itself.*" [4] By the power of the healing Christ, it can be just that.

The death of a patient, therefore, does not signal failure in the ministry of healing. It is failure only when we have not properly prepared people for that healing, when we have not helped them to understand that sometimes only the "medicine of immortality" can make us whole.

Thus, when we pray for healing and the patient is close to death, let us remember that God alone sees the situation in all its ramifications. Edward Bauman reminds us that Augustine's mother prayed fervently that God would prevent her son from journeying to Rome. She was afraid of the evil influences that might claim him there, but while she was praying, his ship sailed. It seemed that her prayers had failed utterly!

In Italy, however, as Bauman reminds us, Augustine met Ambrose and others who turned him "toward the light." Thus," the very conversion for which Monica had prayed took place in the land whose influence she most feared."[5]

So it may be when we pray for wholeness for the dying. It is understandable that we should approach this both with reluctance and ambivalance. These emotions were beautifully expressed in Martin Luther's last words at his daughter's bedside when she had breathed her last, "How strange it is to know that she is at peace and all is well, and yet to be so sorrowful."

CHAPTER 12

Healing and the Positive Mind

This abstract thinker [Hegel] from Stuttgart, coming to Berlin via Jena, thus became the spiritual father of the two most rigid and concrete manifestations of the twentieth century: Prussian militarism and Russian communism. Let nobody doubt the power of ideas.

—*Edward Crankshaw,* The Fall of the House of Hapsburg

The odds were terrifying: a 1-percent chance that his cancer could be cured, a less than 30-percent chance that he would survive the next 5 years, and not even that unless he submitted to intensive chemotherapy. For Bob Gilley, a 41-year-old North Carolina insurance executive, there didn't seem to be much choice. The illness that burst upon his young life without warning was considered a terminal cancer.

This was May 11, 1973, and for the next 10 months Bob Gilley commuted between his home and Houston, Texas, where his chemotherapy was checked and regulated. These were easily the worst 10 months of his life. Like many, Bob Gilley's body reacted violently to the chemotherapy: his hair fell out, most of the time he was nauseated, and his face was ashen with sunken eyes, black rings circling them. He lost 25 pounds and began to look, as he puts it, "like a reject from Dachau."

Then, one day, reading a magazine published by the Unity School of Christianity, he discovered an article about the work of cancer specialist Dr. O. Carl Simonton, of Fort Worth, Texas, who has had unusual success in treating cancer patients with a combination of traditional medical radiotherapy, psychotherapy, and meditation. Looking for a miracle, Bob Gilley dragged himself aboard a flight to Fort Worth.

In his first appointment with Dr. Simonton he told him that he understood he had only a 30-percent chance of survival. "That's right," said Simonton. "What it means is that statistically 70 percent of the people with your disease are going to die and 30 percent are going to live. Which side do you choose?"

Gilley was dumbfounded. "You mean I have a choice?" he asked, incredulous. "You bet your life," the doctor replied. "You're the only one who can make the choice." He went on to describe his approach to combatting the dread disease. The psychotherapy begins with the assumption that the patient shares in the responsibility for his disease. Depression, anxiety, and stress may interfere with the body's normal immune system that fights off disease. Simonton has found that a severe personal trauma—retirement, loss of a mate or family member, loss of a job or demotion, divorce, or some other personal tragedy—often precedes the outbreak of a serious disease by an average of eighteen months. Sometimes the cancer may gain a foothold because the person has unconsciously lost the will to live, has given up on life. So, one of the first things the patient must do is to get in touch with the reasons behind the disease.

A second aspect of the psychotherapy is to "look the beast in the eye without blinking." That means coming face to face with the reality of the cancer and its prognosis. In a sense, one has to face up to the worst before he can concentrate on the best. Too often, Simonton holds, the patient is deceived about the seriousness of the condition or is forced into a conspiracy of silence in which everyone knows but no one is allowed to mention the realities.

If the patient participates in some way in becoming diseased, Simonton believes, then the patient also participates in getting rid of the disease. A very specific approach to that participation is based upon the conviction that we can often learn to gain some measure of control over those functions of the body that are normally under the control of the autonomic nervous system, the portion of our nervous system that normally is not controlled by the conscious mind. Biofeedback, a system of monitoring vital body responses, has pretty well proved that man can learn to

103

control his involuntary, or autonomic, nervous system. For example, Dr. Herbert Benson, an associate professor of medicine at Harvard Medical School and director of the Hypertension Section of Boston's Beth Israel Hospital, tells us that research has demonstrated that "hypertensive *human beings* were capable of lowering their blood pressure." [1]

Dr. Simonton teaches his patients a kind of meditation that has two basic purposes. The first of these is to help the patient to relax through a method known as "progressive relaxation" (to be described in chapter 13). The second is to gain control over the body's disease-fighting forces through a process of visualization (also described in chapter 13). Thus the patient becomes actively engaged in seeking the cure for his disease. For Gilley this was no mere mind-over-matter trick but a kind of prayer in which a person learns to release the power of God within. Everyone has the presence of God within, and must learn how to use it.

Quite against the advice of both his physician and Dr. Simonton, Bob Gilley decided to terminate his chemotherapy treatments. Although he had flown to Fort Worth a desperately ill man who could rarely keep down any solid food, that night he ate Mexican food, and it stayed down. When Bob flew back to North Carolina, his wife was surprised at the change that had come over him: "When he came back, it was like someone had pumped hope into every vein."

Two months after deciding to quit chemotherapy and to begin Dr. Simonton's program, Bob Gilley went to the hospital for tests. Although he felt fine, he was still nervous as he waited for the results. He need not have been anxious, for the doctor's amazed and amazing report was that his disease was gone! Bob Gilley had taken on the 1-percent odds that he could be cured and won. At this writing Bob Gilley is still free of cancer and, as he described himself to me, is "in better health than ever."

Bob Gilley's story—and others like it—would seem to indicate that Dr. Simonton's approach is on the verge of giving us a "miracle cure" for one of our most dreaded diseases. The fact is, as Dr. Simonton himself is quick to point out, Bob Gilley is the exception rather than the rule. But he is the exception not because the system is potentially helpful to only a few, but because many patients simply do not respond with the positive reaction of Bob Gilley. Speaking of Gilley, Dr. Simonton said that "his results are typical for the patient who uses the technique and who has a strong belief system." The problem is that many patients do not have a "strong belief system" or what the religionist calls faith.

When I was a seminary student it was customary to regard Norman Vincent Peale's "positive thinking" with great disdain. "Positive thinking" was a frequent target of the sophisticated theologian and religious journalist. I can well remember how appalled I was in one of my parishes when an elderly woman gave me a stack of Peale's sermons with a testimony of how much they had helped her.

Over the years, however, I have come to realize that, although "positive thinking" can become a distorted emphasis in religion, there is no denying its value in our daily lives. Often a positive, constructive approach may be the key between success and failure, sickness and disease, and even life or death. It is surprising to me now to think that at the same time I was preaching about the need for faith, I was also condemning "positive thinking" as pie-in-the-sky cult of heretical proportions. Closely examining the healings and teachings of Jesus, it is the positive response rather than doctrinal or creedal affirmations that Jesus indicates when he speaks of faith. Nor is the writer of Hebrews thinking of theological formulations or dogma when he says, "Now faith is the assurance of things hoped for, the conviction of things not seen" (Heb. 11:1). And is this not what Paul has in mind when he writes to the Philippians, "Finally, brethren, whatever is true, whatever is honorable, whatever is just, whatever is pure, whatever is lovely, whatever is gracious, if there is any excellence, if there is anything worthy of praise, think about these things" (Phil. 4:8)?

Often in my ministry of healing I have found that people made their disease their whole life. It was what they thought about, talked about, often read about, and were preoccupied with all their waking, and sometimes sleeping, hours. Frequently I found that before they could begin to receive healing there needed to be a radical change of attitude in their lives. Instead of concentrating upon their malady, an understandable but not rewarding preoccupation, I guided them to concentrate upon the wholeness they wanted to achieve. I found that when they shifted their attention away from illness, they often seemed to respond much more to the healing therapy.

Many of the people who came to our healing service were terminal patients, having been told that there was nothing medical that could be done for them. Often, I found, the physician neglected to insert the qualifying term *medical* so that the patient believed that death was inevitable. Perhaps it was only the stubborn life instinct that brought them to our service. They came for spiritual healing because there simply was no other hope.

In his book *Healing, A Doctor in Search of a Miracle,* Dr. William A. Nolen confesses: "It's when the fatal nature of the disease isn't apparent that we doctors have trouble persuading patients, and their families, that *the situation is hopeless"* (italics mine)![2] Why do some physicians feel it is their task to persuade patients that their situation is hopeless? It is not a matter of honesty, for even physicians like Dr. Nolen acknowledge that sometimes their hopeless patients do something extraordinary and live, their physicians' morbid assurances notwithstanding! Professional honesty does not require a physician to convince a patient that the case is "hopeless," only that as far as medicine is concerned—and even the responsibility of making that pronouncement is rather awesome—there is no hope. A doctor can say "There is nothing that I can do for you" or even "I don't know of anyone who can help you" without making the arrogant pronouncement that we have exhausted the resources, not of medical science alone, but of the universe itself.

Perhaps the problem is that we may assume there are but two alternatives: to give the patient a "false" hope and thus be dishonest and irresponsible, or to tell the patient the truth (or rather what we assume the truth to be). In spiritual healing as in

Dr. Simonton's approach we do not give the patient a false hope. Instead, we help the patient face the medical realities and even the possibility of death. I have never promised a patient a cure nor been a party to helping them close their eyes to the medical realities. I have instead helped them to realize that sometimes there are other realities that for the most part we do not understand but are still there for us to try. Having faced the very real possibility of death, without paralyzing fear, the patient has been enabled to "see the glass as half-full instead of half-empty."

A positive approach to healing, therefore, does not mean either dishonesty or a Pollyanna approach to life. It does mean that the patient may be selective in determining those things to which his or her attention will be given. Dr. Philip West, a physician, gives an interesting case study that indicates the strong role that a positive orientation can play in a patient's recovery:

Mr. Wright had a generalized far advanced malignancy involving the lymph nodes. . . . Eventually the day came when he developed resistance to all known palliative treatments. . . . Huge tumor masses, the size of oranges, were in the neck, axillas, groins, chest and abdomen. The spleen and liver were enormous. . . . He was taking oxygen by mask frequently, and our impression was that he was in a terminal state, untreatable, other than to give sedatives to ease him on his way.

In spite of all this, Mr. Wright was not without hope, even though his doctors most certainly were. The reason for this was, that the new drug that he had expected to come along and save the day had already been reported in the newspapers! Its name was "Krebiozen" (subsequently shown to be a useless, inert prepartion [sic]).

Then he heard in some way, that our clinic was to be one of a hundred places chosen by the Medical Association for evaluation of this treatment. We were allotted supplies of the drug sufficient for treating twelve selected cases. Mr. Wright was not considered eligible, since one stipulation was that the patient must not only be beyond where the standard therapies could benefit, but *also* have a life expectancy of at least 3, and preferably 6 months. He certainly didn't qualify on the latter point, and to give him a prognosis of more than 2 weeks seemed to be stretching things.

However, a few days later, the drug arrived, and we began setting up our testing program. . . . When he heard we were going to begin treatment with Krebiozen, his enthusiasm knew no bounds, and as much as I tried to dissuade him, he begged so hard for his "golden opportunity," that against my better judgement, and against the rules of the Krebiozen committee, I decided I would have to include him.

Injections were to be given three times weekly, and I remember he received his first one on a Friday. I didn't see him again until Monday and thought as I came to the hospital he might be moribund or dead by that time. . . .

What a surprise was in store for me! I had left him febrile, gasping for air, completely bedridden. Now, here he was, walking around the ward, chatting happily with the nurses, and spreading his message of good cheer to any who would listen. Immediately I hastened to see the others who had received their first injection at the same time. No change, or change for the worse was noted. Only in Mr. Wright was there brilliant improvement. The tumor masses had melted like snowballs on a hot stove, and in only these few days they were half their original size! . . . Within 10 days he was able to be discharged from his "death-bed," practically all signs of his disease having vanished in this short time. Incredible as it sounds, this "terminal" patient, gasping his last breath through an oxygen mask, was now not only breathing normally, and fully active, he took off in his plane and flew at 12,000 feet, with no discomfort!

Shortly thereafter, reports of other experiments with Krebiozen began to appear in the news media: all with discouraging results. As the weeks wore on, these reports began to take their toll on Mr. Wright. As the reports became even more dismal, Mr. Wright's condition began to deteriorate, and "after two months of practically perfect health, he relapsed to his original state, and became very gloomy and miserable."

But, desiring an opportunity to double-check the drug, as well as to "find out how the quacks can accomplish the results they claim," the physician decided to deceive his patient:

When Mr. Wright had all but given up in despair . . . , I decided to take the chance and play the quack. So, deliberately lying, I told him not to believe what he read in the papers, the drug was really the most promising after all.

The reported failures of the drug with other patients was explained as resulting from poor dosage control. The results of this deception were once more amazing:

Mr. Wright, ill as he was, became his optimistic self again, eager to start over. By delaying a couple of days before the "shipment" arrived, his anticipation of salvation had reached a tremendous pitch. When I announced that the new series of injections were about to begin, he was almost ecstatic and *his faith was very strong* [italics mine].

With much fanfare, and putting on quite an act (which I deemed permissible under the circumstances), I administered the first injection of the doubly potent, *fresh* preparation—consisting of *fresh water* and nothing more. The results of this experiment were quite unbelievable to us at the time, although we must have had some suspicion of the remotely possible outcome to have even attempted it at all.

Recovery from his second near-terminal state was even more dramatic than the first. Tumor masses melted, chest fluid vanished, he became ambulatory, and even went back to flying again. At this time he was certainly the picture of health. The water injections were continued since they worked such wonders. He then remained symptom-free for over two months. At this time the final AMA announcement appeared in the press—"nationwide tests show Krebiozen to be a worthless drug in treatment of cancer."

Within a few days of this report Mr. Wright was re-admitted to the hospital *in extremis*. His faith was now gone, his last hope vanished, and he succumbed in less than two days.[3]

There were people who came to Jesus for healing who, by our enlightened judgments of today, we would say did not correctly believe. One man, a foreigner, knew little about his divinity or messianic role but, because he saw in Jesus authority over disease, received the healing he sought for his servant (see Matt. 8:5). Another, a simple woman, superstitiously believed that if she could just touch the healer's robe, she would be healed, and she was (see Matt. 9:20). Still another, a woman who embraced a hostile faith, believed this man could heal her daughter if only she could persistently seek to persuade him, and she did (see Matt. 15:22). Somehow, it was the tenacity and openness of their belief, not its correctness, that made the healings possible.

Jesus said that if his followers would have faith, they could "move mountains." Often, as Bob Gilley has demonstrated, one of those mountains is our own disease.[4]

CHAPTER 13

A Program for the Patient

"You lack one thing; go, sell what you have, and give to the poor, and you will have treasure in heaven; and come, follow me." At that saying his countenance fell, and he went away sorrowful; for he had great possessions.

—Mark 10:21–22

In my experience in the ministry of healing I have observed two basic reasons some people fail in their search for healing. On the one hand, they do not ask enough of God, and, on the other, they do not ask enough of themselves.

College president Albert Finney was overheard to pray for a long list of persons whose conversion he earnestly desired. Pouring out his heart with a passion for their souls, he ended the prayer saying, "And thou knowest, O Lord, that in these matters I am not accustomed to be denied."

Most of us are probably stunned by such audacity in prayer, particularly those of us who are accustomed to hedging our prayers with customary theological fine print. Yet President Finney's audacity is probably a lot closer to Jesus' teachings on prayer than much of what passes for prayer in Christianity today. We need to remember the unconditional ring of his promises and the *carte blanche* manner in which he responded to people like blind Bartimaeus: "What do you want me to do for you?" Though I know we must be careful of spiritual arrogance, I would agree nevertheless with Emily Gardner Neal when she says, "Our besetting sin, and I think it *is* a sin, is that we habitually expect so pitifully little, daring to impose upon His mercy and His power, the limits of our own humanity." [1]

Many of us also tend to ask far too little of ourselves. Sri Chinmoy, a teacher of meditation, once remarked, "Some people will do anything for their own advancement except work for it."[2] How often I have received in my study a desperate patient exclaiming, "Pastor, I'll do anything to be healed!" And how often I've found that the patient *will* do anything—*except* the very thing or things that are most likely to bring the patient wholeness. Many want a cheap and instant miracle. Only God, however, determines the dispensation of miracles; the healer can only prescribe a program from which a miracle may or may not be forthcoming.

What kind of program can we give to those who seek healing? The following constitutes, not an exhaustive prescription, but merely a suggestive outline.

Seek the Meaning of Your Disease

Illness is often an opportunity for God to tell us something. It is not that he would not want to tell us under other, less troublesome circumstances but that sometimes it is only when we are ill that God can get through to us. Therefore, one of the first things we need to do is to ask God what meaning our illness might have for us, what message it might be trying to communicate to us concerning our physical, emotional, and spiritual life. More than likely, our illness means that there is something out of balance in our lives, some disharmony with which we have not been adequately dealing.

The message may be simple or complex. It might be one of the following:

"You've got to stop smoking!"
"You're eating yourself into the grave!"
"You've got some emotional problems that must be worked out!"
"You've shut yourself off from people!"
"You've got a problem in your marriage!"
"You're trying to hide from God!"
"You're using your sickness to get your own way!"
"You're running away from a painful situation!"
"You've given up on life!"

"You're harboring bitterness (or hatred, jealousy, prejudice) in
   your heart!"

These are but a few of the messages that our illness might give
to us if we were receptive enough. Sometimes we may be able to
hear unaided the message with some honest soul-searching and
prayer. Other times we may need the assistance of a friend,
pastor, or other counselor.

Make Whatever Changes Are Indicated

Frequently, if we listen to what our illness is saying to us, we
will realize that God is calling for some changes in our lives.
Sometimes these changes may be relatively simple, but often what
is called for is a radical overhaul. If our life-style in some way
helps to make us ill or contribute to our sickness, then nothing less
than a sweeping change is likely to be sufficient in order that
healing may occur and be sustained.

Some people will immediately respond: "I can't change. I tried
before and it didn't work!" One of the great potentialities God
places within each of his children is the capacity to change, to
grow, to evolve. What we often mean when we say we "can't
change" is that we don't want to change badly enough; we don't
want to pay the price. Everyone can change if there is a desire to
do so.

This is also true with habits. There isn't any habit that cannot be
broken if we really want to break it. Too many people regard
firmly established habits with an air of fatalism. They assume that
they are fated or doomed to be as they are. But Dr. Arnold
Hutschnecker has put his finger on the problem when he says that
"the difficulty generally is that people think in terms of will
power rather than to consider the power of the established pattern
of their conditioned reflexes and learn to change those."[3]
Circumstances and our own choices tend to establish patterns that
become more rigid as we repeat them. But as patterns can be
formed by our choices, so our patterns can be changed by our
efforts.

The key to a habit is repetition. The more we repeat an act, the more established it becomes. "To break a habit," Hutschnecker says, "repetition is also the key. Each time the habit suggests itself, it must be resisted, and each time it is successfully resisted the habit becomes weaker and the resistance thereafter easier." The making and breaking of habits may be compared to the way a computer is programmed. When we change the input we will begin to change the output as well. "Habits, whether of mind or action, are developed reflexes, and the behavior of a person-ality," says Hutschnecker, "can be considered to be the sum of our conditioned reflexes."[4]

So, we can change either a habit or a whole complex of patterns that makes up our lives. Reflecting upon Pavlov's experiments in conditioned reflexes with dogs, Hutschnecker concludes:

> Through the process of schooling, reading, observation, and thinking, each individual human being develops the pattern of his own specific personality, and through repetition the useful responses become conditioned reflexes.[5]

Develop a Healing Attitude

If you want to receive healing in your life, very likely a radical change in your attitude will be required. Many of us have been conditioned with attitudes toward health that make it very difficult for us to be receptive. As we have previously mentioned, among these harmful attitudes is the belief that perhaps God wills for us to be ill, that we are not good enough to be healed, or that it is unscientific to seek spiritual healing. These attitudes will need to be changed, and one way of helping to change attitudes such as these is to provide ourselves with lots of positive, encouraging input. For years we have saturated ourselves with negative and discouraging input in what we have read, seen in the newspapers, or heard by word of mouth. We can, however, surround ourselves with a different kind of attitude by programming our reading. There are many fine books of faith and encouragement, books about spiritual healing (see the Bibliography at the end of this book), that can have a powerful effect in changing our mind-set and thus our receptivity.

Emmett Fox used to say that just as we are physically what we eat, so we are emotionally and spiritually what we feed ourselves. If we feed our minds a steady diet of cynicism, guilt, despair, and doubt, we will be cynical, guilty, desperate, and doubtful. Our personalities reflect, for the most part, the spiritual and emotional food we feed ourselves daily. By changing our spiritual and mental diet, we can begin to change our outlook and our personalities as well.

Often this will mean changing habits of both thinking and expressing ourselves. If we have made illness (or some tragedy) the focus of our life, we will need to rebuild our lives around something else. For some people, their illness or handicap is their major topic of conversation, their major subject of thought, and the one enduring reality upon which every other phase and activity of their life is dependent. When we have built our lives around an illness, whether long term or short run, we may unconsciously resist being healed because the loss of our illness will mean the loss of our keystone. Furthermore, if the life of the family also centers around that illness, it will be even more difficult to bring healing. Not only will the patient unconsciously resist it, but so too may members of the family who may identify their life's purpose in terms of that one reality.

So, to word it simply (although it is not as simply done), stop thinking about your illness, stop talking about it, and find something else to take its place. Even if pain and disability are constant, you can find something else to occupy center stage—as the blind Helen Keller did, and the deaf Beethoven, as well as Presidents Franklin D. Roosevelt and John F. Kennedy, and Secretary of State Christian Herter, each of them in constant pain or disabilty, yet enormously productive.

Furthermore, stop thinking yourself as "the patient." The more we identify ourselves with that role, the more likely it is to become permanent. Even so slight a matter of changing the present tense to past tense when you refer to your condition can be helpful in disassociating yourself from your illness and thus making it easier to let go of it. Give up the use of the possessive words *my* and *mine*. Stop talking about "my cancer" or "my heart condition." Stop identifying yourself with the condition or the condition with yourself. Some people have difficulty identifying themselves apart from their physical ailment, indicating just how much we may immerse ourselves in the role of the patient.

Visualization is a very effective means of helping us to change our mental outlook. We need to "see" ourselves in the mind's eye exactly as we will look and be when we are completely whole. That visualization can help to strengthen our faith; it is like seeing ourselves, not from the perspective of illness, but through the eyes of faith. We will "see" ourselves as God wants us to be, and we will thank and praise him even before that vision becomes a physical reality. If we act as if it were already true, it more likely will become true because we believe it.

Another aid in changing our mind-set is the use of affirmations. We may use affirmations in two ways. First, we may use them as constant reminders of convictions that we have already accepted intellectually. The ancient Hebrews knew the value of reminding oneself constantly about those things that have already been accepted as items of faith. In Deuteronomy we are told:

> And these words which I command you this day shall be upon your heart; and you shall teach them diligently to your children, and shall talk of them when you sit in your house, and when you walk by the way, and when you lie down, and when you rise. And you shall bind them as a sign upon your hand, and they shall be as frontlets between your eyes. And you shall write them on the doorposts of your house and on your gates. (Deut. 6:6–9)

The idea was: keep these things before you all the time so that they become a part of you. Anyone who is trying to make changes in his life—physical, emotional, spiritual—may profitably use this technique to reinforce his faith. Choose some faith affirmations from the Scriptures and copy them upon some small cards to carry with you, make posters of them and place them in prominent places in your house and your automobile, put them in the medicine cabinet where you keep your razor or lipstick, put

115

them on the mirror where you shave or makeup every day, place them by the bed so that they may be your last thoughts at night and first thought in the morning; the possibilities are endless.

The second use of affirmations will be in your prayers. We will not ask God to make us whole, but we will thank him because he *is* making us whole. We will pray as if we believed his promises and that he is already at work within us.

If we have surrounded ourselves with lots of evidences of our illness, we may also need to make some changes in our environment. Anything around us that reinforces our role as the patient should be removed if at all possible. It may also mean that we may need to be selective in the people with whom we surround ourselves. Some people unconsciously reinforce our negative attitudes and images. They may not mean to, but they help to keep us ill and help to block our recovery.

Build Your Spiritual Support

People who are ill often cut themselves off from the best possible resources for recuperation. Usually there is no better time to strengthen our ties with the church (except in those instances in which a church is more a negative than a positive force—like Job's "friends"). Nor should we wait until we are ill to become better acquainted with the Bible, but there is no better time to do so if along the way we have been neglectful.

Another source of spiritual support may be a prayer or healing group. This may be a group within your own church or another; or it may not be affiliated with one particular congregation. What you are looking for is a group that believes in God's power to heal and will spend some time holding you in intercession.

There may be a healing service conducted somewhere in your own community where you can go for prayer or the laying on of hands. It does not matter whether the healing service is conducted according to your own name-brand faith, so long as you feel God's presence there and believe that God can work through these people for your wholeness.

You may want to write to an organization or healer that carries on intercessory prayer for people needing help and healing. (See note for suggested organizations.)[6] Remember that distance and time are not barriers to intercession, nor are creed and dogma.

Use Meditation as an Aid to Healing

In previous chapters I have indicated the use of meditation as an aid in spiritual healing. The word *meditation* should not cause concern for the Christian, for there is much meditation in the orthodox Christian tradition that is labeled "prayer" or "contemplation." We must not think that the meaning of what the Scriptures call prayer is exhausted by the rather formal and circumscribed practices that prevail in much of our church life today. Jesus sometimes prayed as we do today—verbalized petitions and intercessions—but it is also apparent that sometimes he prayed in different ways for long periods in secluded places.

The style of healing prayer or medication which follows has essentially three purposes: (1) to make us relaxed and receptive; (2) to help us to concentrate; and (3) to enhance the work of the Holy Spirit within us.

Relaxation. I have often found that one of the greatest barriers to healing is the tension and anxiety of the healee. Clench your fist, and I cannot put something into your hand much as I might desire to. But if you relax the hand and let the fist open, the hand assumes a receptive posture, and it can receive whatever gift may be offered.

What is true of the hand is also true of the whole being. Often we cannot receive the gift of God's healing power because we are clenched like the fist. We are too uptight to be receptive to God's healing power. Therefore, we must learn to relax mind, body, and spirit if we would put ourselves into a receptive posture.

Sometimes I have found people improve in their physical condition just through learning the relaxation portion of the meditation by itself. Often, people have spent the better part of their lives being tense and fearful, and the strain on their physical bodies has been enormous.

The first portion of the healing meditation, the "progressive relaxation,'' may be done as follows:

1. Find a quiet, comfortable place if possible.
2. Sit in a comfortable chair, not one that is overstuffed, so that your feet rest on the floor. Back should be straight, head erect but not held stiffly. Hands should be in the lap, palms facing upward if this is comfortable.
3. Turn the head to the left three times—as far as possible without straining—then three times to the right, three times noding forward, three times arching backward. Then, letting the head fall forward to the chest, roll the head three times in a clockwise direction (starting to your left), then three times counterclockwise (starting to your right). As you do this you may hear a crackling sound in your neck, like Rice Krispies. That's all right, it's just an indication that this area where tension is often first recorded is loosening up
4. Close your eyes and sit quietly for a few moments.
5. Take a deep breath, filling the lungs slowly and evenly; then let it out just as slowly and evenly, and as you do, say to yourself, ''Relax, relax, relax.'' Repeat this two times, each time slowly and deeply, letting yourself relax completely.
6. As you continue breathing deeply and slowly, reach out with your mind and ''grasp'' the toes of the left foot. Then, relax the toes and ''let them go'' (in your mind's eye you may see them drifting away effortlessly and painlessly). Do the same with each of the following parts of the body, making sure both that your mind ''feels'' the part named and the part named ''feels'' the grasp of the mind: the left foot, the left lower leg to the knee, the left upper leg and thigh, the left hip, the toes of the right foot, the right foot, the right lower leg, the right upper leg, the right hip, the pubic area, the abdomen, the chest (including the heart, lungs, and esophagus), the small of the back, up the spinal chord, the fingers, hands, lower arms, upper arms and shoulders, the neck, the face, the

back of the skull, the top of the skull (including scalp), and the forehead (Some people find it helpful to tense each of these parts before relaxing them; this is a matter of personal preference.)

7. Continuing to breathe deeply and slowly, you will tell yourself how relaxed your are, almost as if the mind and spirit were floating free of the body.

If you need to relax further add the following: See yourself standing at the top of a long escalator. With your mind's eye, watch both the steps and the railing move down and away from you to the floor below. In your mind's eye "see" and "feel" yourself step on the escalator, and as you count from ten back to zero, "see" and "feel" yourself going down the escalator, stepping off when your count reaches zero.

Visualization of Healing. The following visualizations are helpful in enabling us to respond to God's healing power within us. You may follow the "relaxation" portion of the meditation with one or more of these.

The first technique. As you continue to breathe deeply and slowly, see yourself floating on a fluffy white cloud through a beautiful blue sky. As the cloud continues to float peacefully, it begins to descend slowly, ever so slowly, until at last it touches gently the ground. As you look about you, you see that you have alighted in a beautiful green meadow. The sun is brightly shining and there is an air of peace in the meadow. Looking across the meadow to a far end, you see a group of people. You begin to walk toward the group of people, and, as you come closer, you see a tall figure in the midst of them. As you get closer and closer, you recognize this figure as Jesus, and you see that people are coming to him so that he can place his hands upon them and give them a healing blessing. As you continue walking toward him, you know that you will stand before him, and he will do the same with you. As you finally stand before him, you look up into his face and see the love that radiates from it. Then you will feel his hands on you and the healing power that flows into you and throughout your whole body. Stand before him as long as you feel necessary. If you have a concern for another person, see yourself go and find that person, and bring him or her to stand before Jesus just as you did.

The second technique. In the darkness of your mind's eye, see a tiny pinpoint of golden light as if you were looking down a long, dark tunnel. Move to the light—in reality, Christ—and as you do the point of light gets larger and larger until at last it fills the whole mind's eye. Both see and feel the liquid, golden light of Christ begin to expand from your mind's eye throughout the head, into the neck, and so on, throughout the rest of the body, bit by bit. When the light fills the whole body to the toes, feel and see that light continue to expand beyond your own body to fill the room, the house, the neighborhood, until at last you are joined in that light by the whole world. Know that the light brings wholeness to everything it touches.

The third technique. This is the one used by Dr. Carl Simonton, as mentioned in chapter 12. After you have done the relaxation part of the meditation, visualize the healing forces in your own body attacking the particular physical problem of your own illness. For example: if your illness is leukemia, the white cells outnumbering the red cells of the blood, envision a great red army attacking and defeating a white army. Another patient "saw" a pack of red dogs fighting and subduing a pack of white dogs. If your illness results in a cancerous growth, you might "see" that the healing power of God as a golden liquid dripping from a flask onto the tumor, melting it inch by inch until nothing remains. Another patient, whose pancreas was no longer producing proper amounts of insulin, "saw" an army of construction workers descend upon a house that represented his pancreas, completely renovating it, until it was like new again.

You can use your imagination creatively to visualize your God-given health-defense system working to counteract and defeat your particular disease. Five to ten minutes on this part of the meditation is usually the amount required.[7]

Regardless of which of the visualization techniques you use, you will probably always need to precede them with the relaxation process. As you become more practiced in this, you may need less time for the relaxation portion and may settle down into a relaxed state very quickly. (The relaxation method has often been used helpfully with people who have insomnia.) Together, the relaxation technique and the technique for visualization should be used several times a day.

I entitled this chapter "A Program for the Patient" because I wanted to emphasize the need for the healee to approach healing with the same determined careful planning with which one might plan a first trip abroad, a wedding, or a political campaign. The key word is *discipline,* and the practice is even more remote to many of us than the term itself. Like the little boy who came home with an E on his report card, we would have to confess that discipline is our worst subject.

Some years ago Adlai Stevenson said that "the United States has lost impetus and conviction because it has confused the free with the free and easy."[8] Assured that we are "saved by the free grace of God," many Christians have also confused the "free" with "the free and easy." Proud of our freedom, we proclaim, "Nobody tells us what to believe or do!" And the "nobody" includes ourselves. Least of all do *we* tell ourselves what to do.

The ministry of spiritual healing, with few exceptions, is free—but it is not free and easy! If we want healing, we must decide upon a program as if our life depended upon it—for it very well may! As Robert Raines puts it: "We must lay hands of gentle ruthlessness on ourselves, eliminating some things in order to intensify others. It is necessary to prune our lives if they are to bear more fruit."[9]

121

CHAPTER 14

Why Not in Your Church?

The doctor and the minister can be so involved in dispensing their "standardized" solutions to people's problems that they allow the more personal aspects of their ministry to go undone. Such persons as have been mentioned are ready prey for cultic groups that emphasize faith healing, all out of proportion to common sense, intelligent medical practice, or sound religious teaching.

—Wayne Oates, "The Pastor and Faith Healing," Religion and Health

While I was writing this book I was advised that it would be more attractive to publishers if I were to aim it more at the "secular audience and not so much the church crowd." The advice was probably quite sound, but, although I did not intend to address only "the church crowd," one of my purposes from the very beginning has been to make a strong argument for the healing ministry to lay and clergy alike so that we may stop relegating this ministry to the church's back door.

For too long, many of the clergy have taken the attitude of refusing to give this ministry even a second thought. Father Francis MacNutt tells us of a Roman Catholic priest of his acquaintance who took this attitude. The priest, who liked to use dramatic effects with his sermons, told Father MacNutt that on a weekend retreat with a group of college students whom he considered a difficult audience, in order to emphasize that "they should not look for emotional highs or for proofs" of faith, he decided to begin his sermon with a tongue-in-cheek "spiel on faith healing (in which he did not believe)." He told his students that he possessed the gift of healing and invited them to come forward to the altar to receive it. Thirty students responded to his bogus invitation.

His plan was to pray for them and "then when they weren't healed, he could say, 'You see! You were fooled! You are looking for miracles. Our faith is not like that. . . . You are not to be seeking signs and wonders.'"

Copying what he had seen Oral Roberts do on television, he prayed only in sham and pretense, expecting nothing to happen. But his plans went awry: "You know what happened? They were all healed—or seemed to be. The headaches I can explain; they were cured by the power of suggestion in my sermon. But there was one boy with his arm in a sling who went back to his pew waving his arm and claiming he was cured; that bothered me. I was really glad next day when one student did come back to say she still had swelling in her sprained ankle which she had thought was cured. But all those other students acted as if they were healed. It spoiled the whole point of my sermon." [1]

I trust that in these years ahead God is going to spoil a lot of sermons and change a lot of minds and hearts within the churches. It is time for the churches to radically change their stance in regard to the ministry of healing. Morton T. Kelsey sees two different and conflicting attitudes in the Christian churches today toward the ministry of healing, a ministry, Kelsey reminds us, "that was practically unbroken for the first thousand years of the church's life." One of these attitudes is one of increasing interest among some Christians. The other, however, he sees as an "actual hostility to the practice of healing—hostility even to the idea of it." The churches are still obsessed, he says, "with the materialistic conviction that man's body can be cared for by medical and physical means alone and that religious help is superfluous." [2]

There are still other churchmen, I believe, who take a different attitude. It is a "that's-nice-if-you-like-that-kind-of-thing" attitude. Spiritual healing has become a popular subject for secular and even for some religious magazines, an interesting topic for the churches' equivalent of the cocktail hour, a fringe option for those who are not entirely satisfied with the mainstream of church life.

I'm not sure whether that is progress. I'm not certain whether it is better to have people mildly titillated by it or outright hostile to it, for indifferent tolerance comes no closer to its imperative than outright rejection. This book is no mere plea for tolerance by the churches. It is an appeal to restore the ministry of healing to its rightful place in the life and mission of the church.

Nor should there be any misunderstanding to the nature of that ministry. I am not speaking of the admission that God sometimes heals people in rare instances. This is the familiar concept of a God who on rare occasions does something supernatural, intervening in the natural order and overriding it, bringing down a gift from heaven for the occasional man or woman with the requisite faith or worthiness.

No, I am speaking of a ministry that does not attempt to change or bend God's will, but concentrates upon changing our own responsiveness to his healing purpose. I am speaking of a supernormal ministry, a ministry that deals with God-given natural powers which as yet lie beyond our understanding. I am talking about a ministry that knows no "one right way" or technique but sees the healing power mediated in different ways or models:

—a healing "energy" transmitted by touch or prayer that enables the Holy Spirit within us to enhance the body's own God-given power to regenerate and heal itself either with or without medicine

—a healing attitude transmitted from the healer to the healee (or the intercessor to the intercessee) that frees the body to function as God created it to do

—a supportive act, or attitude, in counseling, preaching, or teaching that calls forth psychological or spiritual adjustments that need to be made if the body's own immune system is to function

—a discipline of self-therapy—physical, psychological, and spiritual

—a program of prayer, meditation, reading, and personality reform that mobilizes the whole person's resources for wholeness

124

And where is God in these pictures? God is in the world of energy and forces which he creates and sustains. He is in the concern and skill of the friend and the professional. God is in the therapies and medicines of the physician, the surgeon, the pharmacist, the psychiatrist, the dentist, etc. And God is in the wonderful self-repair system of each human body, the hands of the healers, and the prayers of the intercessors.

My appeal to the church is a recapitulation of much that has already been said in this book.

First, I would call the churches to remember that the ministry of spiritual healing is at the very heart of the gospel of Jesus Christ as we find it in both the New Testament and the early church. It is a saving/healing gospel that cannot but be truncated when we ignore this aspect.

We need to return to the Gospels and view once again the place that ministry played in Jesus' own mission. As R. K. Harrison reviews that ministry for us in *The Interpreter's Dictionary of the Bible,* we are reminded:

> Instead of manifesting an attitude of contempt toward the weak and the sick, Jesus showed in his first recorded sermon that his earthly ministry was closely bound up with the frail and feeble of body and soul.
>
> [He] never once supported the OT concept of disease as a punishment sent by God. Instead, he frequently envisaged the incidence of disease as the result of evil producing an imbalance within the personality.[3]

Harrison reminds us that it was Cartesian philosophy that divided the personality of man into physical and mental categories, "considering the latter alone the proper sphere of operation of the church."

> [Jesus] disavowed entirely the idea that sickness was sent by God as a punitive measure, nor did he encourage the belief that the sufferer ought to remain ill in order to acquire courage or learn patience. . . . Fundamental to all his healing activity was his conviction that disease was not an established part of the divine order of things. . . .
>
> These healings cannot be explained satisfactorily on the simple assumption that he was a shrewd psychologist who dismissed a

wide variety of psycho-neurotic conditions by means of adroit techniques which were in advance of contemporary practice. While psychological theories can throw much light on the healing work of Jesus, they cannot of themselves explain it fully.[4]

The gospel of Jesus Christ is a message and power of healing for broken bodies, broken spirits, broken lives, broken families, broken communities, and a broken world. We cannot truly appreciate the significance of that gospel if we ignore the healing perspective.

Second, the command of Christ to preach, teach, *and heal* has never, as far as I am aware, been repealed and it remains a compelling imperative for his followers today. We have been very long on the teaching, longer still on the preaching, but very lacking on the healing.

Third, we need to restore the healing ministry to the churches today because we are concerned about the whole man and have a wholistic faith. A church that is concerned only with the "disembodied" souls of men is neither faithful to the commission of Christ nor fruitful in its mission.

Fourth, if the churches continue to ignore the Christian ministry of healing, they will only further help to consign healing to the cults and the fringe groups where its meaning may be distorted and misunderstood. When a legitimate gift of the Spirit does not find adequate expression within the established churches, it will find recipients beyond the fringe. The occult is the manifestation, not so much of the devil's dark strategems, as of the rejection of the Spirit's gifts by the churches.

Fifth, if we are truly concerned about people, we cannot afford to ignore a ministry that has brought help and comfort to so many people. There are many things that the churches cannot do for people, but here is a resource that is within the reach of any congregation.

Sixth, the ministry of spiritual healing may be an important contribution that the churches may make to modern medicine. Some believe that medicine has become one of the most secularized branches of science. Therefore, there is a need for the churches to make a contribution and witness in this field once again. The churches need to consider re-entering the field of public health. I truly regret that, although many fine hospitals owe their conception and growth to the outreach of the churches, most of these have become completely secularized as if there was no longer a relationship beyond the annual appeal for benevolence funds.

Finally, I regard the ministry of spiritual healing as a channel for the demonstration of God's power in an age that seems largely unresponsive to talk alone. To be sure, some people may become devotees of spiritual healing because they become hooked on the spiritual fireworks. But it is equally lamentable to have to admit that there are so many congregations that have never experienced any "fireworks" at all. And let's not rationalize that away by saying that we don't need any, that faith doesn't need any demonstration. Jesus' ministry contained an abundance of signs and wonders, and these continued well into the early church. In fact, whenever the church has been renewed or reformed, there have always been requisite signs and wonders manifested, not as a steady diet, but frequently enough so that churchmen were not afraid of them or unable to recognize them when they did occur.

Several months ago I was teaching a six-week course in spiritual healing at a suburban United Methodist church. It was the third session of the course, and I had previously mentioned a few times the use of healing meditation in my ministry. So, I decided to conclude the session with a brief demonstration of how the meditation could be used.

I guided them through the relaxation portion of the meditation, and then we did the visualization of Jesus healing in the meadow (as outlined in chapter 12). After finishing the meditation, I dismissed the class and prepared to gather up my things and leave. While I was doing this, a young woman came to me with a quizzical look on her face. "You know," she said, "I think something happened to my hip during that meditation." Somewhat preoccupied with what I was doing, I smiled and said, "Oh, that's nice. I'm glad." "But I really mean it," she

127

persisted, her voice rising suddenly in a mixture of glee and surprise. "I believe my hip is really healed!"

Looking up from my activities, I said, "Barbara that's great. I am really very thankful." Barbara glowed and hurried down the hall while I went back to what I was doing, Later, after church, I saw her again, and she called to me across the crowd of worshipers, "Look, I'm not limping!" I remember thinking how ironic it was that I had only intended to demonstrate the healing meditation technique, not to do any healing.

Later that week I got a call from Barbara. "You probably don't know the importance of what happened on Sunday morning," she said. Without waiting for me to admit that I probably didn't, she went on to tell me that she had severely injured the hip almost a year ago in a very bad fall at a church retreat. Ever since, she had great discomfort and was unable to walk without limping. Nothing her doctor had done seemed to help her. Recently he had told her that if there was no improvement soon, she would have to have surgery, and there was no guarantee even with the surgery.

Until that Sunday morning, she said, there had not been improvement. If anything, she seemed to have more difficulty. But from the moment we began the healing meditation that morning, she knew that something was happening. When it was over there was no pain nor any impediment. After church, she told me, she had actually run up and down the hall to demonstrate her healing to her amazed friends.

Two very important results came from that unexpected healing: (1) the limb was restored for Barbara's use and comfort and (2) there was also a witness to the power of God for both Barbara and the congregation and even beyond. About a week later I got a call from a local radio personality who had heard of Barbara's healing and wanted the two of us to appear on his "open-mike" program in which listeners can call in to comment or ask questions. Consequently, Barbara, her pastor, and I spent a full hour talking with listeners about God's power to heal the sick and the broken. From this little class in a suburban church there came an opportunity for witness and evangelism to the larger community.

128

I believe the time has come for theological seminaries to join in the research and to provide training for seminarians in this field, for denominations and judicatories to bring seminars and workshops into the local churches, for local ministers and congregations to inaugurate healing missions and regularly scheduled healing services, for lay persons to be instructed in spiritual healing and sent forth with at least as much determination invested in the building-fund campaign or the Every Member Canvass.

This ministry which Cyril Richardson calls "a *token* of the Resurrection," may represent the power of the kingdom of God breaking forth anew. It may be seen, says Richardson, as "an aspect of realized eschatology . . . a breaking-through of powers to be realized in the future, when death shall be swallowed up in victory."[5] It is unthinkable that the churches should fail to provide the opportunity for this to occur. In his translator's preface to *The Young Church in Action* (the book of Acts), J. B. Phillips observes:

> Whatever conclusions our modern conferences may reach, there can be no reasonable doubt that the early Church possessed the power to heal and even to raise the dead. . . . That the Church today has very largely lost this power of healing the sick is undeniable, although it is heartening to know that in recent years Christians all over the world are not content to accept this loss as the inevitable price we must pay for the march of Science.[6]

That was written in 1955, approximately a decade before I began my ministry of healing. It was certainly the attitude that seemed to prevail all about me, but I have seen a slow and subtle change taking place. Clergy who once slipped into the back of the sanctuary to view the healing service and then slip away like Nicodemus "by night," began to come and stay with greater frequency. Another United Methodist pastor, William A. Kreichbaum, began to assist me on Thursday mornings and began a healing service in his own church on Wednesday evenings. A local physician came from time to time and participated in the laying on of hands at the altar. Ministerial groups asked me to come and talk about the ministry, as did many more service clubs and civic associations. A nurses' organization asked me to speak on this subject and was very receptive (I have found nurses more receptive as a vocational group than any other). Opportunities came to speak in various churches and forums across the United States. Newspaper articles appeared. People began to write and ask for help from all over the United States, South America, Canada, Mexico, Europe, Israel, and Africa. One entire family from Puerto Rico came for a whole week, staying in a local motel room so that they could attend the healing service. A retired California physician suffering from cancer got on a transcontinental train and came to Pennsylvania to share in our ministry. The Annual Conference of The United Methodist Church to which I belong asked the bishop to appoint a committee to study spiritual healing, a study that I understand is still continuing. (We excel at making studies in the church, reminding me of Murray Kempton's observation that as our crises get worse, our reports about them get better!) And everywhere I go, speaking with other clergy and lay persons involved in the ministry of healing, the report is much the same: despite the critics, the hostility of the materialists, the resistance from the churches, the suspicion by members of the medical profession, there is a change taking place and the ministry of spiritual healing is gaining in acceptance—even in churches!

It is said that when Bernard of Clairvaux made his one visit to Rome, the Pope delighted in showing this rustic man the gleaming splendors and riches of the Vatican. At last, referring to Peter's reply to the blind man at the Temple in Acts 3—"I have no silver and gold, but I give you what I have; in the name of Jesus Christ of Nazareth, walk"—the Pope points to the wealth of the church and says, "Ah, Bernard, no longer must the Holy Church say, 'Silver and gold have I none'!" "Yes, Holy Father," replied Bernard softly, "but neither can we any longer say, 'Take up thy bed and walk'!"

Bernard may have been right on that occasion, but I think he might have to make another retort today. By the power of God, the church is on the threshold of recovering her gift of healing.

Notes

Chapter 1.

1. General letter from Lawrence W. Althouse to participants in his ministry of healing.
2. Private correspondence to the author.
3. Private correspondence to the author.

Note: Throughout the book I have changed the names of healees in order to protect their privacy.

Chapter 2.

1. Kelsey, *Healing and Christianity* (New York: Harper & Row, 1973), p. 147.
2. Ibid., pp. 196, 198.
3. MacNutt, *Healing* (Notre Dame, Ind.: Ave Maria Press, 1974), p. 73.
4. Alan Richardson, *A Theological Word Book of the Bible* (New York: The Macmillan Co., 1955), p. 103.
5. Ibid., p. 104.
6. Tillich, *The Journal of Pastoral Counseling,* 6 (Fall-Winter, 1971-72), p. 4n.
7. Father Secondo Mazzarello quoted in "Sacrament for the Sick," *Time* (February 5, 1973), p. 65.

Chapter 3.

1. Kelsey, *Healing and Christianity* (New York: Harper & Row, 1973), p. 65.
2. Ibid., pp. 59, 89.
3. Neal, *The Lord Is Our Healer* (Englewood Cliffs, N.J.: Prentice-Hall, 1961), p. 73.
4. Ibid., p. 31.
5. Paul Tournier, *The Meaning of Persons* (New York: Harper & Brothers, 1957), pp. 90–91.
6. Ian G. Barbour, "The Significance of Teilhard," *The Christian Century* (August 30, 1967), p. 1098.

Chapter 4.

1. Teilhard de Chardin, *Hymn of the Universe* (New York: Harper & Row, 1969), p. 90.
2. Bett, *The Reality of Religious Life* (New York: The Macmillan Co., 1949), p. 82.
3. Ibid., pp. 61, 63.

Chapter 5.

1. Kramer, *Instant Replay: The Green Bay Diary of Jerry Kramer* (New York: New American Library, 1968), p. 43.
2. Hutschnecker, *The Will to Live* (New York: Cornerstone Library, 1972), p. 21.
3. Paul Tournier, *The Meaning of Persons* (New York: Harper & Brothers, 1957), p. 186.
4. Servadio, *Unconscious and Paranormal Factors in Healing and Recovery* (London: Society for Psychical Research, 1963), p. 18.
5. Hutschnecker, *The Will to Happiness* (New York: Cornerstone Library, 1972), pp. 141-43.
6. Stanley Krippner and Alberto Villoldo, *The Realms of Healing* (Millbrae, Calif.: Celestial Arts, 1976), p. 269.

7. Ibid., p. 268.

8. Klopfer, "Psychological Variables in Human Cancer," *Journal of Projective Techniques* (1957), p. 339.

9. Millet, "Body, Mind, and Spirit," in *Religion and Health,* ed. Simon Doniger (New York: Association Press, 1958), pp. 34-36.

Chapter 6.

1. Bruce Larson, *Dare to Live Now* (Waco, Tex.: Word Books, 1965), p. 62.

2. Richardson, "Spiritual Healing in the Light of History," in *Religion and Health,* ed. Simon Doniger (New York: Association Press, 1958), p. 55.

3. Ibid., p. 57.

4. Turner, *An Outline of Spiritual Healing* (London: Psychic Press, 1961), p. 16.

5. Richardson, "Spiritual Healing," p. 63.

Chapter 7.

1. Nolen, *Healing: A Doctor in Search of a Miracle* (New York: Random House, 1974), p. 308.

2. Grad and Paul Cadoret, "An Unorthodox Method of Treatment on Wound Healing in Mice," *International Journal of Parapsychology,* 3 (Spring, 1964), pp. 5–24; Grad, "Some Biological Effects of the Laying on of Hands: A Review of Experiments with Animals and Plants," and "The 'Laying on of Hands': Implications for Psychotherapy, Gentling, and Placebo Effect," *Human Dimensions,* 5:27-45.

3. Ibid.

4. Smith, "Enzymes Are Activated by the Laying on of Hands," and "Paranormal Effects on Enzyme Activity," ibid., pp. 46–51.

5. Turner, "Some Experiments in Healing," paper, p. 8.

6. Ibid.

7. Miller, "Paraelectricity: A Primary Energy," *Human Dimensions,* 5: 22–26; Brame and Douglas Dean, "Physical Changes in Water by Laying-on-of-Hands," *Proceedings: Second International Conference on Psychotronic Research* (Paris: Institut Metaphysique, 1975).

8. Miller and P. B. Reinhart, "Measuring Psychic Energy," *Psychic* (May–June, 1975).

9. Miller, "The Positive Effect of Prayer on Plants," ibid. (April, 1972).

10. Miller, "Paraelectricity: A Primary Energy," pp. 25, 26.

11. A personal interview with Dr. Edward Brame.

12. Krieger, "Healing by the 'Laying-On' of Hands as a Facilitator of Bioenergetic Change: The Response of In-vivo Human Hemoglobin," *Psychoenergetic Systems,* 1 (1976), forthcoming.

13. Graham and Anita Watkins, "Possible PK Influence on the Resuscitation of Anesthetized Mice," *Journal of Parapsychology* (1971), pp. 35, 257-72; Graham and Anita Watkins and R. A. Wells, "Further Studies on the Resuscitation of Anesthetized Mice," *Research in Parapsychology,* ed. W. G. Roll, R. L. Morris, and J. D. Morris (Metuchen, N.J.: Scarecrow Press, 1973).

14. Stanley Krippner and Alberto Villoldo, *The Realms of Healing* (Millbrae, Calif.: Celestial Arts, 1976), p. 34.

15. Thelma Moss, *The Probability of the Impossible* (J. P. Tarcher, Inc., 1974), chap. 2.

16. Ibid., pp. 43–51, 60.

17. John O. Pebeck, David L. Faust, and Harry J. Kyler, *Science Magazine,* as quoted in the *Wall Street Journal,* October 12, 1976; William A. Tiller, *Research Reports* (Stanford, Calif.: Stanford University Department of Material Science, 1975).

Chapter 8.

1. Bernard S. Via, Jr., "Alternative to Healing," *The Christian Advocate* (July 10, 1969).

2. Hutschnecker, *The Will to Happiness* (New York: Cornerstone Library, 1974), p. 16.

3. Ibid., p. 78.

4. Ibid., p. 79.

5. Ibid.

Chapter 9.

1. Hutschnecker, *The Will to Live* (New York: Cornerstone Library, 1974), p. 21.

2. Laurence J. Peter, *The Peter Principle: Why Things Always Go Wrong* (New York: William Morrow & Co., 1969).

3. Tournier, *The Meaning of Persons* (New York: Harper & Brothers, 1957), p. 146.

4. Lewis, *Surprised by Joy: The Shape of My Early Life* (New York: Harcourt, Brace & Co., 1955), p. 189.

5. Hutschnecker, *The Will to Live,* p. 100.

Chapter 10.

1. Harry Edwards, "Have I Found Faith?" (The Sanctuary, Shere, Guildford, Surrery, England).

2. Milne, "A Doctor's Witness," *The Churches' Handbook for Spiritual Healing,* ed. Walter W. Dwyer (New York: Ascension Press, 1962), p. 12.

3. Neal, *The Lord Is Our Healer* (Englewood Cliffs, N.J.: Prentice-Hall, 1962), p. 56.

4. Spraggett, *Kathryn Kuhlman: The Woman Who Believes in Miracles* (New York: World Publishing Co., 1970).

5. White, *Christian Life and the Unconscious* (New York: Harper & Brothers, 1955), p. 17.

Chapter 11.

1. Hammarskjöld, *Markings* (New York: Alfred A. Knopf, 1964), p. 82.

2. Kübler-Ross, *On Death and Dying* (New York: The Macmillan Co., 1969), pp. 6, 7.

3. Jacks, quoted in *A Diary of Readings,* ed. John Baillie (New York: Charles Scribner's Sons, 1955), p. 36.

4. Letter to the author.

5. Teilhard de Chardin, *Hymn of the Universe* (New York: Harper & Row, 1969), p. 104.

6. Bauman, *Intercessory Prayer* (Philadelphia: The Westminster Press, 1971), p. 41.

Chapter 12.

1. Benson, *The Relaxation Response* (New York: William Morrow & Co., 1975), p. 79.

2. Nolen, *Healing: A Doctor in Search of a Miracle* (New York: Random House, 1974), p. 5.

3. Bruno Klopfer, "Psychological Variables in Human Cancer," *Journal of Projective Techniques* (1957), pp. 337–39.

4. The sources of all information on Bob Gilley in this chapter are a personal interview with Mr. Gilley and an article by Pat Bordon in the May 2, 1976, issue of *The Charlotte Observer*.

Chapter 13.

1. Emily Gardner Neal, *The Lord Is Our Healer* (Englewood Cliffs, N.J.: Prentice-Hall, 1961), p. 116.

2. Lawrence LeShan, *How to Meditate: A Guide to Self-Discovery* (Boston: Little, Brown, 1974), p. 96.

3. Hutschnecker, *The Will to Happiness* (New York: Cornerstone Library, 1974), p. 67.

4. Ibid., pp. 68, 69.

5. Ibid., p. 74. For those who need help in changing patterns and breaking habits, I recommend Dr. Hutschnecker's book *The Will to Happiness or How to Make and Break Habits* by Jhan Robbins and Dale Fisher.

6. Organizations that are willing to receive names for intercessory prayer include the following:

Spiritual Frontiers Fellowship, 10715 Winner Road, Independence, Missouri 64052 Telephone: 816-254-8585

Unity School of Christianity, Unity Village, Missouri 64065 Telephone: 816/524-5104

Oral Roberts, Prayer Tower, Tulsa, Oklahoma Telephone: 918/492-7777

The Upper Room Prayer Service, 1908 Grand Avenue, Nashville, Tennessee 37202

7. A cassette tape containing this technique, "A Healing Meditation," by Larry Althouse is available for $5 from Star Productions, 632 South Locust Street, Elizabethtown, Pennsylvania 17022.

8. Robert Raines, *New Life in the Church* (New York: Harper & Row, 1961), p. 56.

9. Raines, *Reshaping the Christian Life* (New York: Harper & Row, 1964), p. 134.

Chapter 14.

1. Francis MacNutt, *Healing* (Notre Dame, Ind.: Ave Maria Press, 1974), pp. 131–32.

2. Morton T. Kelsey, *Healing and Christianity* (New York: Harper & Row, 1973), pp. 6, 9.

3. Harrison, "Healing," in *The Interpreter's Dictionary of the Bible*, Vol. E-J (Nashville: Abingdon Press, 1962), p. 546.

NOTES

4. Ibid., p. 547.

5. Cyril Richardson, "Spiritual Healing in the Light of History," in *Religion and Health* (New York: Association Press, 1958), pp. 60, 61.

6. Phillips, *The Young Church in Action* (New York: The Macmillan Co., 1955), pp. xv, xvi.

Bibliography

Barbour, Ian, ed. *Science and Religion*. New York: Harper & Row, 1968.

Bett, Henry. *The Reality of Religious Life*. *New Perspectives on the Dialogue*. The Macmillan Co., 1949.
Toward a contemporary understanding of science and religion.

Hammond, Sally. *We Are All Healers*. New York: Harper & Row, 1973.
A good, if somewhat uncritical, survey of healing in the United States and England.

Higgins, Paul Lambourne, ed. *Frontiers of the Spirit*. Minneapolis, Minn.: T. S. Dennison, 1976.
Healing within the context of the parapsychological and paranormal perspectives of religion.

Hutschnecker, Arnold. *The Will to Live*. New York: Cornerstone Library, 1972.
_____ . *The Will to Happiness*. New York: Cornerstone Library, 1972.
Excellent books by a physician for the lay reader on the emotional dimensions of sickness.

Kelsey, Morton T. *Healing and Christianity*. New York: Harper & Row, 1973.
The most thorough book on healing from the perspectives of Christian scripture, history, and theology.

Kimmel, Jo. *Steps to Prayer Power*. Nashville: Abingdon Press, 1972.
Creative prayer techniques effective for those seeking wholeness.

Krippner, Stanley, and Villoldo, Alberto. *Realms of Healing*. Millbrae. Calif.: Celestial Arts, 1973.
Healing examined at length by two parapsychologists.

LeShan, Lawrence. *The Medium, the Mystic and the Physicist: Toward a General Theory of the Paranormal*. New York: Ballantine Books, 1975.
Chapters 7–9 record significant experiments with psychic healing.

Lovett, C. S. *Jesus Wants You Well!* Calif.: Personal Christianity, 1973.
Creative approach to healing from a fundamentalist perspective.

MacNutt, Francis. *Healing*. Notre Dame, Ind.: Ave Maria Press, 1974.
Healing from the point of view of a Roman Catholic priest and healer.

Melton, J. Gordon. *A Reader's Guide to the Church's Ministry of Healing*. Independence, Mo.: The Academy of Religion and Psychical Research (1973), 10715 Winner Road.
A comprehensive annotated bibliography on healing and its related fields.

Moss, Thelma, *The Probability of the Impossible*. Los Angeles: J. P. Tarcher, 1974.
  Chapters 1–4 give a view on healing by an eminent parapsychologist. Also available in paperback.
Neal, Emily Gardner. *A Reporter Finds God Through Spiritual Healing*. Minneapolis: Macalester Press, 1960.
––––––– . *The Lord Is Our Helper*. Englewood Cliffs, N.J.: Prentice-Hall, 1968.
  Excellent studies of healing by a newspaper reporter who set out to discredit healing and ended up in the healing ministry herself.
Parker, William R., and St. Johns, E. *Prayer Can Change Your Life*. Englewood Cliffs, N.J.: Prentice-Hall, 1957.
  Prayer techniques by a clinical psychologist. Also in paper.
Rindge, Jean Pontius, ed. "Approaches to Healing: Laying on of Hands," *Human Dimensions, 5*.
  Detailed reports of healing research by leading healers and parapsychologists.
Sanford, Agnes. *The Healing Light*. Minn.; Macalester Park, 1957.
  A personal approach to healing by a noted healer. Also in paper.
Shealy, Norman. *Occult Medicine Can Save Your Life: A Modern Doctor Looks at Unconventional Healing*. New York: Dial Press, 1975.
  Good approach by a surgeon despite an unfortunate title.
Sherman, Harold. *Your Power to Heal*. New York: Fawcett, 1972.
  Covers a wide range of perspectives and experiences.
Spraggett, Allen. *Kathryn Kuhlman: The Woman Who Believes in Miracles*. New York: World Publishing Co.
  An in-depth study of a reknowned charismatic healer.
Tournier, Paul. *The Healing of Persons*. New York: Harper & Brothers, 1955.
––––––– . *The Meaning of Persons*. New York: Harper & Brothers, 1957.
  Spiritual factors in medicine by a noted Christian physician.
Weatherhead, Leslie. *Psychology, Religion, and Healing*. Nashville-New York, Abingdon-Cokesbury Press, 1951.
  A pioneer who links healing with both psychology and religion.
White, Ernest. *Christian Life and the Unconscious*. New York: Harper & Brothers, 1955.
  Unconscious factors in spiritual and mental wholeness.
Whitehead, Alfred North. *Science and the Modern Mind,* New York: Mentor, 1959.
  A twentieth-century scientific world view.
Worrall, Ambrose A., with Olga N. *The Gift of Healing*. New York: Harper & Row, 1965.
––––––– . *Explore Your Psychic World*. New York: Harper & Row, 1970.

The experience and technique of healing by two of America's most
gifted healers and interpreters. The first book is their personal story;
the second is a report of a seminar with them and notable scientists.

Other Resources
Especially for the Cancer Patient (but not exclusively)

Dr. O. Carl Simonton of Oncology Associates, Forth Worth, Texas (a
medical doctor and cancer expert), has had remarkable success in
treating cancer patients with a combination of chemotherapy,
psychotherapy, and meditation. This approach is explained in a set of
cassette tapes and brochure available from Cognetics, Inc., P.O. Box
592, Saratoga, California 95070. (Or call Mr./Mrs. Motis at
408-252-5754.) Send $25 and ask for Simonton Packet.

APPENDIX A

A SERVICE OF HEALING

Before the Service: May we prepare ourselves in silence. "Thou dost keep him in perfect peace whose mind is stayed on thee."

I. WORDS OF PREPARATION:

"Come to me, all who labor and are heavy laden, and I will give you rest."

"For where two or three are gathered in my name, there am I in the midst of them."

"My peace I give to you."

"Ask, and it will be given you; seek, and you will find; knock, and it will be opened to you."

"If you ask anything in my name, I will do it."

II. A PRAYER OF INVOCATION: (Minister and People)

Almighty God, unto whom all hearts are open, all desires known, and from whom no secrets are hid, cleanse the thoughts of our hearts by the inspiration of thy Holy Spirit, that we may perfectly love thee and worthily magnify thy holy name; through Jesus Christ our Lord, who hath taught us when we pray to sap in me dried up as in a summer drought.

III. THE ACT OF CONFESSION:

"While I refused to speak, my body wasted away with moaning all day long. For day and night thy hand was heavy upon me, the sap in me dried up in a summer drought.

Then I declared my sin, I did not conceal my guilt.

I said, 'With sorrow I will confess my disobedience to the Lord'; then thou didst remit the penalty of my sin." (Psalms 32:3-5, NEB)

A Prayer of General Confession: (Minister and people) Almighty and most merciful Father; we have erred and strayed from thy ways like lost sheep. We have followed too much the devices and desires of our own hearts. We have offended against thy holy laws. We have left undone things which we ought to have done; and we have done those things which we ought not to have done; and there is no health in us. But thou, O Lord, have mercy upon us miserable offenders. Spare thou us, O God, who confess our faults. Restore thou those who are penitent; according to thy promises declared unto us in Christ Jesus our Lord. And grant, O most merciful Father, for his sake, that we may hereafter live godly, righteous, and sober life, to the glory of thy holy name. Amen.

The Assurance of Pardon: If we confess our sins he is faithful and just, and will forgive our sins and cleanse us from all unrighteousness.

IV. A HYMN OF PRAISE

V. A SCRIPTURE READING

VI. A MEDITATION ON THE HEALING MINISTRY

VII. A PERIOD OF INTERCESSION

"Is any among you suffering? Let him pray . . . Is any among you sick? Let him call for the elders of the church, and let them pray over him . . . and the prayer of faith will save the sick man, and the Lord will raise him up." (James 5:13-15)

We are met together here as members of Christ's Body, the Church, commissioned to do his healing work on earth. Let us remember that his healing life will flow through us, his channels, to those in need. Let us claim with strong confidence the promise made to all intercessors: " . . . whatever you ask in prayer, believe that you receive it, and you will."

VIII. THE MINISTRY OF THE LAYING ON OF HANDS

Let us now sit back, relaxed and comfortable. Then, with eyes closed, let us gently and trustfully repeat the words of this healing promise: GOD'S HEALING LOVE IS WITHIN ME. Let us sit in silence for a few moments until the invitation to come forward is given.

When the invitation is given, you may come forward, one at a time, kneeling at the altar rail to receive the laying-on-of hands for forgiveness of sin, healing of mind, body, and spirit, personal problems and concerns, either for yourself or others.

Those desiring not to kneel may come forward and sit in the front pew instead.

IX. A PRAYER OF PRAISE AND THANKSGIVING—The Doxology (congregation joining)

X. THE BENEDICTION " . . . your faith has made you well; go in peace, and be healed of your disease."

The seminar and healing services are part of the ministry of this church and are supported entirely from its budget. No offerings will be received.

Remember:

God alone is the healer.

It is important to cooperate with your doctor and follow his directions. Do not take it upon yourself to cease his prescribed medications and treatments. Let him pronounce you well.

Regularly give thanks and substance in your own chosen place of worship.

No one can promise a healing. As Olga Worrall, a lay healer of long experience has put it:

> The minister or layworker and the congregation or group are joining forces in trying to create the right atmosphere for holding communion with God thru Christ, in the hope that if every condition is met with, a healing may take place. Instantaneous healings are extremely rare, so don't expect them. And above all, don't be disturbed if nothing happens for weeks or months on end. The healing services will not have been in vain. Every person who has attended the services will have received spiritual food for the soul. Remember, often the soul is healed first before the healing can manifest itself thru the physical body. Have faith expectancy; remember that healings take place in God's time and not man's time.

Practice these five steps:

1. Relax your body so that all tension goes out of you.
2. Free your mind and let God fill it with his presence.
3. Let yourself be cleansed of all fear, resentment, anxiety, and guilt.
4. Visualize what you desire. See yourself or the person from whom you are interceding free from all pain, sickness, or distress.
5. Thank God for his gift even before you have received it.

> "The healing of His seamless dress
>   Is by our beds of pain;
> We touch Him in life's throng and press
>   And we are whole again."
> —Whittier

APPENDIX B

A Letter on the Healing Ministry

Dear Friend,

I appreciate your recent inquiry concerning my ministry of spiritual healing. Because of the large volume of requests for assistance, I cannot answer each letter personally, although I would prefer to do so.

First, I want to affirm the keystone conviction upon which my healing ministry is based: God alone is the Healer and we are but instruments used to accomplish his purpose. Therefore, the emphasis must be upon the Source of Healing, not the instrument or channel. God uses many people to accomplish this purpose of his healing ministry: doctors, nurses, surgeons, pastors, lay persons.

Secondly, we operate on the conviction that God's will for us is wholeness, not disease or brokenness. Jesus never indicated to anyone that he could not or would not heal them because God intended for them to remain ill. As in many areas of life, there are many obstacles that may interfere with God's will—human sin, doubt, unreceptivity, fear, and unhealthy habits—but be assured that God wants you whole . . . even more than you do!

Next, we believe that this wholeness for which God creates us is a wholeness of mind, body and spirit. Thus we treat the whole person, not just sick organs or bodies or sick minds. Although we all seek healing of the physical body, the healing of the spirit we recognize as the highest form and ultimate goal of the healing ministry.

I cannot promise the results you look for, only that I will do my best, confident in the knowledge of the many people who have been greatly helped by this ministry. I do believe that everyone who seeks help through the ministry of healing can receive healing of the spirit and often the spirit must experience healing before the body can. Sometimes, however, we must realize that in asking for wholeness it may be given either through physical recovery or through that process we call death. We must leave to His wisdom which of these is indicated as most beneficial to the patient. Death should not be regarded as the ultimate tragedy, but as the *ultimate healing*. All physical healing, whether by medical science or spiritual healing, is temporary.

The ministry of healing, it must be emphasized, is not in competition with medical science. We believe it is important to co-operate with your physician and we encourage you not to take it upon yourself to terminate prescribed medications or therapies. Let your physician pronounce you well.

Next, please understand that, although they do occur sometimes, instantaneous healings are quite rare; more often, spiritual therapy like medical therapy, will likely require time and perseverance. It often requires weeks, months, and years for us to get into a pattern of disease or impairment and we must be willing to allow sufficient time to be freed of that pattern.

It is important for you to realize that it is not necessary for the patient or intercessor to be physically present to receive the benefits of this healing ministry. The healing force is unlimited by time and space. Healing can be sent just as effectively from here as by your bedside.

At your request I will place your name or the name of the patient for whom you wish to serve as intercessor on my special Healing list for one month from the date I receive the request. These names may be renewed for successive one-month intervals by additional requests. I will appreciate a card or note informing me of the patient's progress. But please note: *the patient's name must be renewed each month.*

Those whom I see personally are taught a prayer-meditation technique to help them in receiving healing. I recommend that it be used three times daily. If you are interested in securing a copy of this technique, it is now available on cassette tape and can be ordered from:

Star Productions
632 South Locust Street
Elizabethtown, Pennsylvania 17022

(Specify the ''Althouse Healing Tape'' and send a check for $5). This tape can be particularly helpful to those seeking healing from a distance.

I would also advise you to inquire about churches holding healing ministries in your local area. A call to the local council of churches office may be helpful in locating a church. Also, you might contact the closest chapter of Spiritual Frontiers Fellowship to inquire whether that organization has a healing ministry in your area. (See the enclosed resource list for the address of the national office of SFF.)

I do not make it a practice to travel in order to administer healing, since healing may be just as effective with me remaining here, as explained above. From time to time, however, I am available to conduct healing services and/or speak on healing where there is sufficient interest. My desire is to see many more churches involved in this ministry. Neither do I encourage people to come long distances to Dallas for healing. It is not necessary.

Proper preparation for healing, whether by the laying on of hands or by petitionary or intercessory prayer, is very important. A minimal preparation should include the following steps:

1. Relax your body so that all tension leaves you.
2. Free your mind so that God may fill it with his presence.
3. Let yourself be cleansed by God of all fear, worry, resentment, hostility, or guilt.
4. Visualize what you desire (which is also what God wills). See yourself (or the person for whom you are interceding) as free from all pain, sickness, and distress and full of life, strength, and peace.
5. Thank God expectantly for this gift even before it is received.

Healing is more likely to take place through submission to God than by our own efforts. It is not a matter of getting Him to agree to what we desire, but letting Him accomplish in us what he desires. If there are barriers to healing, it is with us, not Him.

Finally, if you are seeking healing, please be honest with yourself and *be sure you want to be whole!* Some people unconsciously hold onto sickness and unhappiness because they do not want to accept the responsibilities of life that health entails. Sometimes, too, people are ill because of an unconscious desire to punish themselves. Being whole means being an aware and responsible person. What will you do with your wholeness if God grants it to you?

There is no fee or charge for this ministry of healing although it is appreciated if you send a postage-paid and self-addressed envelope for replies. If you want to contribute a nominal amount to assist with mailing and handling, you may do so. But please: *If you are helped by this ministry of healing, do not send money to me, but make a thank-offering of some kind in the church or charity of your choice.*

God bless you,

Lawrence W. Althouse